Praise for Adam Kahane's book

Transformative Scenario Planning

"I highly commend this book. Adam has taken scenario planning to a new level, beyond the confines of business strategy, to deal with wider social and economic issues."
—**Vince Cable, Secretary of State for Business, United Kingdom**

"All of our toughest problems, from climate change to inequality, have complexity at their heart. Adam Kahane, with his track record of work for social and environmental justice, has written a powerful and practical guide for those hungry for new ideas about how to achieve change."
—**Phil Bloomer, Director, Campaigns and Policy, Oxfam**

"We all face challenges and opportunities that can only be addressed with fresh understandings and innovative forms of collaboration. At Shell we have learned the value of combining scenario thinking with strategic choices. Building on his extensive practical experience, Kahane extends the boundaries of this practice."
—**Jeremy Bentham, Vice President, Global Business Environment, Royal Dutch Shell**

"This deeply human book offers tangible means for tackling the intractable problems that confront us at every level of life, from domestic and local to national and beyond. It offers realistic, grounded hope of genuine transformation, and its insights and lessons should be part of the toolbox of everyone in leadership roles."
—**Thabo Makgoba, Anglican Archbishop of Cape Town**

Power and Love

"This profound book offers us a wise way to negotiate our toughest group, community, and societal challenges."
—**William Ury, Senior Fellow, Harvard Negotiation Project, and coauthor of** *Getting to Yes*

"This is a rare and valuable book. Kahane has immersed himself in the practical challenges of helping people effect social change, and against this backdrop he unfolds a simple and penetrating insight: that power and love are two axes that delineate our individual and collective journeys. Either we master the balance of power and love

or we will fail in our efforts to realize deep and lasting change."
   —**Peter Senge, Senior Lecturer, Massachusetts Institute of Technology, and author of** *The Fifth Discipline*

"In *Power and Love*, Adam goes further and deeper into the kind of leadership that it takes to do this. A must-read for every reflective leader."
   —**Ravi Vankatesan, former Chairman, Microsoft India**

"Kahane is a master practitioner and thinker who knows the highs and lows of solving some of the toughest problems of social discord. *Power and Love* is both instructive and inspiring."
   —**Patrick Dodson, Founding Chairman, Council for Aboriginal Reconciliation**

"*Power and Love* should be read and reread by anyone seriously committed to addressing tough problems."
   —**Morris Rosenberg, Deputy Minister of Foreign Affairs, Government of Canada**

Solving Tough Problems

"This breakthrough book addresses the central challenge of our time: finding a way to work together to solve the problems we have created."
   —**Nelson Mandela**

"A seminal book. Exciting, vital, essential reading."
   —**Edgar H. Schein, Professor of Management Emeritus, Massachusetts Institute of Technology Sloan School of Management, and author of** *Process Consultation*

"Our societies face really hard problems—poverty, injustice, sustainability, corruption—that are insoluble by conventional means. Conflicts of interest and profound uncertainties about the future are producing paralysis and inaction. Adam Kahane has, more than anyone, developed and successfully employed tools that enable us to create futures of shared progress and profit."
   —**Peter Schwartz, Senior Vice President for Government Relations and Strategic Planning, Salesforce.com, and author of** *The Art of the Long View*

"This book should be read by everyone who is concerned with the quality of decision making in our democracies."
   —**Elena Martinez, former Assistant Secretary General, United Nations**

TRANSFORMATIVE SCENARIO PLANNING

OTHER BOOKS BY ADAM KAHANE
Solving Tough Problems: An Open Way of Talking, Listening, and Creating New Realities
Power and Love: A Theory and Practice of Social Change

Transformative Scenario Planning

WORKING TOGETHER TO CHANGE THE FUTURE

Adam Kahane

A Reos Partners Publication

Berrett–Koehler Publishers, Inc.
San Francisco
a BK Currents book

Berrett-Koehler Publishers, Inc.
235 Montgomery Street, Suite 650
San Francisco, CA 94104-2916
Tel: (415) 288-0260   Fax: (415) 362-2512   www.bkconnection.com

Ordering Information
Quantity sales. Special discounts are available on quantity purchases by corporations, associations, and others. For details, contact the "Special Sales Department" at the Berrett-Koehler address above.
Individual sales. Berrett-Koehler publications are available through most bookstores. They can also be ordered directly from Berrett-Koehler: Tel: (800) 929-2929; Fax: (802) 864-7626; www.bkconnection.com
Orders for college textbook/course adoption use. Please contact Berrett-Koehler: Tel: (800) 929-2929; Fax: (802) 864-7626.
Orders by U.S. trade bookstores and wholesalers. Please contact Ingram Publisher Services, Tel: (800) 509-4887; Fax: (800) 838-1149; E-mail: customer.service@ingrampublisherservices.com; or visit www.ingrampublisherservices.com/Ordering for details about electronic ordering.

Berrett-Koehler and the BK logo are registered trademarks of Berrett-Koehler Publishers, Inc.

Printed in the United States of America
Berrett-Koehler books are printed on long-lasting acid-free paper. When it is available, we choose paper that has been manufactured by environmentally responsible processes. These may include using trees grown in sustainable forests, incorporating recycled paper, minimizing chlorine in bleaching, or recycling the energy produced at the paper mill.

Library of Congress Cataloging-in-Publication Data
Kahane, Adam.
Transformative scenario planning : working together to change the future / Adam Kahane. -- 1st ed.
    p. cm.
Includes bibliographical references.
ISBN 978-1-60994-490-2 (pbk.)
1. Conflict management. 2. Social problems. 3. Social change. 4. Social planning. 5. Cooperation. 6. Problem solving. 7. Social sciences--Simulation methods. I. Title.
HM1126.K343 2012
658.3'145--dc23
                              2012024104

First Edition
15 14 13 12   10 9 8 7 6 5 4 3 2 1

Interior design: Laura Lind Design   *Cover design:* Pemastudio
Copy editor: Elissa Rabellino   *Proofreader:* Henrietta Bensussen
Production: Linda Jupiter Productions   *Indexer:* Linda Webster

To Dorothy

Contents

Foreword
by Kees van der Heijden

*W*HENEVER LIFE BECOMES MORE HECTIC and uncertain, scenario planning becomes more popular. This empirical fact is not surprising. Scenario planning is in the first place a diagnostic tool for conditions in which uncertainty rules. Experience shows that the tool delivers; in most scenario planning exercises, people experience "aha" moments about the problematic situation they are facing. Even so, the scenario client is often left with a feeling of dissatisfaction, as it seems difficult to directly attribute action in the world to the scenario work done. It seems that important new insights gained often do not compete very successfully when the scenario planner returns to the daily work situation, where the old logics reestablish themselves around him or her. In situations of anxiety around issues in the environment, people want to see something more directly emerging from their attempts to cope with the problematic situation.

Adam Kahane thinks that scenario planning should be able to do better. He has explored the limitations of current practice and how these can be overcome in a world experiencing an increasing number of big and growing problem situations to which as yet we lack a suitable response. His conclusions are powerful in their simplicity and plausibility. He observes that while finding and sharing a rational diagnosis of the situation is a key element of any successful coping behavior, it is generally not enough for change to happen. He identifies two additional important components that scenario work needs to incorporate for it to become a more significant contributor toward real coping in a turbulent world: (1) the big issues of our days need to become a more central part of people's personal identity and value systems; and (2) counteracting the increasing turbulence requires more focus on mobilizing autonomous system forces.

Adam Kahane's reasoning continues a long tradition in social system theory. In the 1960s, Emery and Trist introduced the concept of the "turbulent environment" where massive change undermines our confidence in our ability to cope. Prigogine explained the experienced increase in turbulence as a consequence of denser connectivity in the environment as more increasingly mobile people live closer together and affect each other. More connections means more closed loops and therefore more positive feedback loops driving self-reinforcing change. The recent credit crisis is just one example.

At the Saïd Business School at the University of Oxford, we have been pursuing this line of thinking. This work has been published in the context of an ongoing series of conferences, called the Oxford Futures Forum. Our work indicates that survival in a turbulent environment requires a new response based on mobilizing the same systemic forces that generate the turbulent change in the first place. In trying to cope, we must fight like with like. That means that successful coping involves building feedback loops in the environment that can counteract the destructive autonomous loops that cause the turbulence we experience. Adam Kahane refers to this as the seeds planted by the scenario work multiplying and spreading. His observations over many years of reflective practice confirm what the theory suggests here.

In summary: In a turbulent world, successful coping requires activity in three focus areas: (1) systemic diagnosis of the situation and its context, (2) network development to enable self-reinforcing coping behavior, and (3) personal identification with the project. Scenario planning has proved itself as a successful diagnostic tool. Adam Kahane shows how consciously dealing with the developing turbulent environment now additionally requires focus on the development of self-triggering networks and personal values.

This book puts these issues on the agenda and provides us with ideas generated in the world of practice, requiring our individual and organizational attention. The world has two options. We can wait, hoping and trusting that we, or the next generation, will find some way out when the situation becomes untenable. Or we can try to anticipate and change direction by proactively improving our coping skills. If we choose the latter, Adam Kahane provides an important perspective.

Preface

$\mathcal{E}$ACH OF US MUST CHOOSE, in each situation, how we will approach the future. Sometimes we choose to accept what is happening around us and try to adapt ourselves to it. Other times we choose to challenge what is happening and try to change it. This is the choice that Reinhold Niebuhr pointed to in his much-loved maxim: "Lord grant me the serenity to accept the things I cannot change, the courage to change the things I can, and the wisdom to know the difference."

If we choose to try to change the future, then we must choose how. More often than not, we choose to push. We have an idea of the way we think things ought to be, and we marshal our resources—arguments, authority, supporters, money, weapons—to try to make it so. But often when we push, others push back, and we end up frustrated, exhausted, and stuck. Over and over we encounter such stuck situations, in all kinds of social systems: families, teams, communities, organizations, nations.

This book is for people who have chosen to try to change the future and have realized that they cannot do so unilaterally. They may be trying to change the future of their city or their country or the world; they may be focusing on health or education or the economy or the environment; they may be acting from a position in business or government or civil society. This book is for these people, who are looking for a way to work together—

not only with friends and colleagues but also with strangers and opponents—and so to be able to get unstuck and move forward and create change.

I first got a glimpse of such a new way of working with the future twenty years ago, during the transition away from apartheid in South Africa. I was unexpectedly plunged into working with a team of leaders from all parts of South African society—black and white, left and right, opposition and establishment—who were trying to construct a better future for their country. I saw, in what they were doing and how they were doing it, a brief and clear image of this new way—like a nighttime landscape momentarily illuminated by a flash of lightning. I knew that I had seen something important, but I didn't quite know what it was or where it had come from or how it worked. I have spent the past twenty years working on understanding what I saw. This book reports what I have learned.

Over these past two decades, my colleagues and I have worked with hundreds of teams of people who are working together to change the future. These teams have tackled some of the most important and difficult challenges of our time: health care, economic development, child nutrition, judicial reform, social inclusion, food security, and climate change, across the Americas, Europe, the Middle East, Africa, Asia, and Australia. They have included politicians, peasants, activists, artists, academics, businesspeople, trade unionists, civil servants, and leaders of community, youth, indigenous, and religious organizations. Some of these teams have been local and others global; some have worked together for days and others for years; some have succeeded in changing their situation and others have failed.

Through these experiences, I have learned that it *is* possible for people who are in a situation they want to change—people who need each other in order to get unstuck and move forward but who don't understand or agree with or trust one another—to work together cooperatively and creatively to effect that change. And I have learned the what and why and how of this approach.

My colleagues and I call this new way of working *transformative scenario planning*. Its purpose is to enable those of us who are trying to change the future collaboratively to *transform*, rather than adapt to, the situation we are part of. It involves a transformation of the situation—like a caterpillar into a butterfly—rather than only an incremental or temporary change. We bring this about through transforming our own thoughts and actions and our relationships with others. Transformative scenario planning centers on constructing *scenarios* of possible futures for our situation, but it takes the well-established adaptive scenario planning methodology and turns it on its head—so that we construct scenarios not only to understand the future but also to influence it.[1] And it involves *planning*, not in the sense of writing down and following a plan, but in the sense of engaging in a disciplined process of thinking ahead together and then altering our actions accordingly.

Transformative scenario planning offers us a new way to work together to change the future. This new way is simple, but it is not easy or straightforward or guaranteed. It requires learning how to make a specific series of steps, but also, perhaps more important, making a profound and subtle shift in how we approach one another and the situations of which we are part. Above all, it requires practicing: learning by doing. This book outlines this new way and invites you into the doing.

1

An Invention Born of Necessity

ON A LOVELY FRIDAY AFTERNOON in September 1991, I arrived at the Mont Fleur conference center in the mountains of the wine country outside of Cape Town. I was excited to be there and curious about what was going to happen. I didn't yet realize what a significant weekend it would turn out to be.

THE SCENARIO PLANNING METHODOLOGY MEETS THE SOUTH AFRICAN TRANSFORMATION

The year before, in February 1990, South African president F. W. de Klerk had unexpectedly announced that he would release Nelson Mandela from 27 years in prison, legalize Mandela's African National Congress (ANC) and the other opposition parties, and begin talks on a political transition. Back in 1948, a white minority government had imposed the apartheid system of racial segregation and oppression on the black majority, and the 1970s and 1980s had seen waves of bloody confrontation between the government and its opponents. The apartheid system, labeled by the United Nations a "crime against humanity," was the object of worldwide condemnation, protests, and sanctions.

1

Now de Klerk's announcement had launched an unprecedented and unpredictable process of national transformation. Every month saw breakthroughs and breakdowns: declarations and demands from politicians, community activists, church leaders, and businesspeople; mass demonstrations by popular movements and attempts by the police and military to reassert control; and all manner of negotiating meetings, large and small, formal and informal, open and secret.

South Africans were excited, worried, and confused. Although they knew that things could not remain as they had been, they disagreed vehemently and sometimes violently over what the future should look like. Nobody knew whether or how this transformation could happen peacefully.

Professors Pieter le Roux and Vincent Maphai, from the ANC-aligned University of the Western Cape, thought that it could be useful to bring together a diverse group of emerging national leaders to discuss alternative models for the transformation. They had the idea that the scenario planning methodology that had been pioneered by the multinational oil company Royal Dutch Shell, which involved systematically constructing a set of multiple stories of possible futures, could be an effective way to do this. At the time, I was working in Shell's scenario planning department at the company's head office in London. Le Roux asked me to lead the meetings of his group, and I agreed enthusiastically. This is how I came to arrive at Mont Fleur on that lovely Friday afternoon.

My job at Shell was as the head of the team that produced scenarios about possible futures for the global political, economic, social, and environmental context of the company. Shell executives used our scenarios, together with ones about what could happen in energy markets, to understand what was going on in their unpredictable business environment and so to develop more robust corporate strategies and plans. The company had used this *adaptive scenario planning* methodology since 1972, when a brilliant French planning manager named Pierre Wack constructed a set of stories that included the possibility of an unprecedented interruption in global oil supplies. When such a crisis did in fact occur in 1973, the company's swift recognition of and response to this industry-transforming event helped it to rise from being the weakest of the "Seven Sisters" of the international oil industry to being one of the strongest. The Shell scenario department continued to develop this methodology, and over the years that followed, it helped the company to anticipate and adapt to the second oil crisis in 1979, the collapse of oil markets in 1986, the fall of the Soviet Union, the rise of Islamic radicalism, and the increasing pressure on companies to take account of environmental and social issues.[1]

I joined Shell in 1988 because I wanted to learn about this sophisticated approach to working with the future. My job was to try to understand what was going on in the world, and to do this I was to go anywhere and talk to anyone I needed to. I learned the Shell scenario methodology from two masters: Ged Davis, an English mining engineer, and Kees van der Heijden, a Dutch economist who had codified the approach that Wack invented. In 1990, van der Heijden was succeeded by Joseph Jaworski, a Texan lawyer who had founded the American Leadership Forum, a community leadership development program that was operating in six US cities. Jaworski thought that Shell should use its scenarios not only to study and adapt to the future but also to exercise its leadership to help shape the future. This challenged the fundamental premise that our scenarios needed to be neutral and objective, and it led to lots of arguments in our department. I was torn between these two positions.

Wack had retired from Shell in 1980 and started to work as a consultant to Clem Sunter, the head of scenario planning for Anglo American, the largest mining company in South Africa. Sunter's team produced two scenarios of possible futures for the country as an input to the company's strategizing: a "High Road" of negotiation leading to a political settlement and a "Low Road" of confrontation leading to a civil war and a wasteland.[2] In 1986, Anglo American made these scenarios public, and Sunter presented them to hundreds of audiences around the country, including de Klerk and his cabinet, and Mandela, at that time still in prison. These scenarios played an important role in opening up the thinking of the white population to the need for the country to change.

Then in 1990, de Klerk, influenced in part by Sunter's work, made his unexpected announcement. In February 1991 (before le Roux contacted me), I went to South Africa for the first time for some Shell meetings. On that trip I heard a joke that crystallized the seemingly insurmountable challenges that South Africans faced, as well as the impossible promise of all their efforts to address these challenges together. "Faced with our country's overwhelming problems," the joke went, "we have only two options: a practical option and a miraculous option. The practical option would be for all of us to get down on our knees and pray for a band of angels to come down from heaven and solve our problems for us. The miraculous option would be for us to talk and work together and to find a way forward together." South Africans needed ways to implement this miraculous option.

THE MONT FLEUR SCENARIO EXERCISE

Necessity is the mother of invention, and so it was the extraordinary needs of South Africa in 1991 that gave birth to the first transformative scenario planning project.[3] Le Roux and Maphai's initial idea was to produce a set of scenarios that would offer an opposition answer to the establishment scenarios that Wack and Sunter had prepared at Anglo American and to a subsequent scenario project that Wack had worked on with Old Mutual, the country's largest financial services group. The initial name of the Mont Fleur project was "An Alternative Scenario Planning Exercise of the Left."

When le Roux asked my advice about how to put together a team to construct these scenarios, I suggested that he include some "awkward sods": people who could prod the team to look at the South African situation from challenging alternative perspectives. What le Roux and his coorganizers at the university did then was not to compose the team the way we did at Shell— of staff from their own organization—but instead to include current and potential leaders from across the whole of the emerging South African social-political-economic system. The organizers' key inventive insight was that such a diverse and prominent team would be able to understand the whole of the complex South African situation and also would be credible in presenting their conclusions to the whole of the country. So the organizers recruited 22 insightful and influential people: politicians, businesspeople, trade unionists, academics, and community activists; black and white; from the left and right; from the opposition and the establishment. It was an extraordinary group. Some of the participants had sacrificed a lot—in prison or exile or underground—in long-running battles over the future of the country; many of them didn't know or agree with or trust many of the others; all of them were strong minded and strong willed. I arrived at Mont Fleur looking forward to meeting them but doubtful about whether they would be able to work together or agree on much.

I was astounded by what I found. The team was happy and energized to be together. The Afrikaans word *apartheid* means "separation," and most of them had never had the opportunity to be together in such a stimulating and relaxed gathering. They talked together fluidly and creatively, around the big square of tables in the conference room, in small working groups scattered throughout the building, on walks on the mountain, on benches in the flowered garden, and over good meals with local wine. They asked questions of each other and explained themselves and argued and made jokes. They agreed on many things. I was delighted.

The scenario method asks people to talk not about what they predict *will* happen or what they believe *should* happen but only about what they think *could* happen. At Mont Fleur, this subtle shift in orientation opened up dramatically new conversations. The team initially came up with 30 stories of possible futures for South Africa. They enjoyed thinking up stories (some of which they concluded were plausible) that were antithetical to their organizations' official narratives, and also stories (some of which they concluded were implausible) that were in line with these narratives. Trevor Manuel, the head of the ANC's Department of Economic Policy, suggested a story of Chilean-type "Growth through Repression," a play on words of the ANC's slogan of "Growth through Redistribution." Mosebyane Malatsi, head of economics of the radical Pan-Africanist Congress (PAC)—one of their slogans was "One Settler [white person], One Bullet"— told a wishful story about the Chinese People's Liberation Army coming to the rescue of the opposition's armed forces and helping them to defeat the South African government; but as soon as he told it, he realized that it could not happen, so he sat down, and this scenario was never mentioned again.

Howard Gabriels, an employee of the Friedrich Ebert Stiftung (the German social democratic foundation that was the primary funder of the project) and a former official of the socialist National Union of Mineworkers, later reflected on the openness of this first round of storytelling:

> The first frightening thing was to look into the future without blinkers on. At the time there was a euphoria about the future of the country, yet a lot of those stories were like "Tomorrow morning you will open the newspaper and read that Nelson Mandela was assassinated" and what happens after that. Thinking about the future in that way was extremely frightening. All of a sudden you are no longer in your comfort zone. You are looking into the future and you begin to argue the capitalist case and the free market case and the social democracy case. Suddenly the capitalist starts arguing the communist case. And all those given paradigms begin to fall away.[4]

Johann Liebenberg was a white Afrikaner executive of the Chamber of Mines. Mining was the country's most important industry, its operations intertwined with the apartheid system of economic and social control. So in this opposition-dominated team, Liebenberg represented the arch-establishment. He had been Gabriels's adversary in acrimonious and violent mining industry negotiations and strikes. Gabriels later recalled with amazement:

> In 1987, we took 340,000 workers out on strike, 15 workers were killed, and more than 300 workers got terribly injured, and when I say injured, I do not only mean little scratches. He was the enemy, and here I was, sitting with this guy in the room when those bruises are still raw. I think that Mont Fleur allowed him to see the world from my point of view and allowed me to see the world from his.[5]

In one small group discussion, Liebenberg was recording on a flip chart while Malatsi of the PAC was speaking. Liebenberg was calmly summarizing what Malatsi was saying: "Let me see if I've got this right: 'The illegitimate, racist regime in Pretoria . . .'" Liebenberg was able to hear and articulate the provocative perspective of his sworn enemy.

One afternoon, Liebenberg went for a walk with Tito Mboweni, Manuel's deputy at the ANC. Liebenberg later reported warmly:

> You went for a long walk after the day's work with Tito Mboweni on a mountain path and you just talked. Tito was the last sort of person I would have talked to a year before that: very articulate, very bright. We did not meet blacks like that normally; I don't know where they were all buried. The only other blacks of that caliber that I had met were the trade unionists sitting opposite me in adversarial roles. This was new for me, especially how open-minded they were. These were not

people who simply said: "Look, this is how it is going
to be when we take over one day." They were prepared
to say: "Hey, how *would* it be? Let's discuss it."[6]

I had never seen or even heard of such a good-hearted and
constructive encounter about such momentous matters among
such long-time adversaries. I wouldn't have thought it was possible, but here I was, seeing it with my own eyes.

In the following six months, the team and I returned to Mont
Fleur for two more weekend workshops. They eventually agreed
on four stories about what could happen in the country—stories
they thought could stimulate useful debate about what needed
to be done. "Ostrich" was a story of the white minority government that stuck its head in the sand and refused to negotiate with
its opponents. "Lame Duck" was a story of a negotiated settlement that constrained the new democratic government and left
it unable to deal with the country's challenges. "Icarus" was a
story of an unconstrained democratic government that ignored
fiscal limits and crashed the economy. "Flight of the Flamingos"
was a story of a society that put the building blocks in place to
develop gradually and together.[7]

One of the team members created a simple diagram to show
how the scenarios were related to one another. The three forks in
the road were three decisions that South African political leaders (who would be influenced by people such as the members
of the Mont Fleur team) would have to make over the months
ahead. The first three scenarios were prophetic warnings about
what could happen in South Africa if the wrong decisions were
made. The fourth scenario was a vision of a better future for
the country if all three of these errors were avoided. When they
started their work together, this politically heterogeneous team
had not intended to agree on a shared vision, and now they were
surprised to have done so. But both the content of the "Flight of
the Flamingos" scenario and the fact that this team had agreed
on it served as a hopeful message to a country that was uncertain and divided about its future.

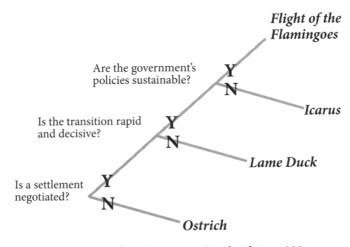

The Mont Fleur Scenarios, South Africa, 1992

The team wrote a 16-page summary of their work that was published as an insert in the country's most important weekly newspaper. Lindy Wilson, a respected filmmaker, prepared a 30-minute video about this work (she is the one who suggested using bird names), which included drawings by Jonathan Shapiro, the country's best-known editorial cartoonist. The team then used these materials to present their findings to more than 100 political, business, and nongovernmental organizations around the country.

THE IMPACT OF MONT FLEUR

The Mont Fleur project made a surprisingly significant impact on me. I fell in love with this collaborative and creative approach to working with the future, which I had never imagined was possible; with this exciting and inspiring moment in South African history, which amazed the whole world; and with Dorothy Boesak, the coordinator of the project. By the time the project ended in 1993, I had resigned from Shell to pursue this new way of working, moved from London to Cape

Town, and married Dorothy. My future was now intertwined with South Africa's.

The project also made a surprisingly significant impact on South Africa. In the years after I immigrated to South Africa, I worked on projects with many of the country's leaders and paid close attention to what was happening there. The contribution of Mont Fleur to what unfolded in South Africa, although not dramatic or decisive, seemed straightforward and important. The team's experience of their intensive intellectual and social encounter with their diverse teammates shifted their thinking about what was necessary and possible in the country and, relatedly, their empathy for and trust in one another. This consequently shifted the actions they took, and these actions shifted what happened in the country.

Of these four scenarios, the one that had the biggest impact was "Icarus." The title of the story referred to the Greek mythical figure who was so exhilarated by his ability to fly using feathers stuck together with wax that he flew too close to the sun, which melted the wax and plunged him into the sea. In his book on Mont Fleur and the two prior South African corporate-sponsored scenario exercises, economist Nick Segal summarized the warning of "Icarus" about the dangers of macroeconomic populism as follows:

> A popularly elected government goes on a social spending spree accompanied by price and exchange controls and other measures in order to ensure success. For a while this yields positive results, but before long budgetary and balance of payment constraints start biting, and inflation, currency depreciation and other adverse factors emerge. The ensuing crisis eventually results in a return to authoritarianism, with the intended beneficiaries of the programme landing up worse off than before.[8]

This scenario directly challenged the economic orthodoxy of the ANC, which in the early 1990s was under strong pressure from its constituents to be ready, once in government, to borrow and spend money in order to redress apartheid inequities. When members of the scenario team, supported by Mboweni and Manuel, presented their work to the party's National Executive Committee, which included both Nelson Mandela (president of the ANC) and Joe Slovo (chairperson of the South African Communist Party), it was Slovo, citing the failure of socialist programs in the Soviet Union and elsewhere, who argued that "Icarus" needed to be taken seriously.

When le Roux and Malatsi presented "Icarus" to the National Executive Committee of the Pan-Africanist Congress—which up to that point had refused to abandon its armed struggle and participate in the upcoming elections—Malatsi was forthright about the danger he saw in his own party's positions: "This is a scenario of the calamity that will befall South Africa if our opponents, the ANC, come to power. And if they don't do it, we will push them into it." With this sharply self-critical statement, he was arguing that his party's declared economic policy would harm the country and also its own popularity.

One of the committee members then asked Malatsi why the team had not included a scenario of a successful revolution. He replied: "I have tried my best, comrades, but given the realities in the world today, I cannot see how we can tell a convincing story of how a successful revolution could take place within the next ten years. If any of you can tell such a story so that it carries conviction, I will try to have the team incorporate it." Later, le Roux recalled that none of the members of the committee could do so, "and I think this failure to be able to explain how they could bring about the revolution to which they were committed in a reasonable time period was crucial to the subsequent shifts in their position. It is not only the scenarios one accepts but also those that one rejects that have an impact."[9]

This conversation about the scenarios was followed by a full-day strategic debate in the committee. Later the PAC gave up their arms, joined the electoral contest, and changed their economic policy. Malatsi said: "If you look at the policies of the PAC prior to our policy conference in September 1993, there was no room for changes. If you look at our policy after that, we had to revise the land policy; we had to revise quite a number of things. They were directly or indirectly influenced by Mont Fleur."[10]

These and many other debates—some arising directly out of Mont Fleur, some not—altered the political consensus in the opposition and in the country. (President de Klerk defended his policies by saying "I am not an ostrich."[11]) When the ANC government came to power in 1994, one of the most significant surprises about the policies it implemented was its consistently strict fiscal discipline. Veteran journalist Allister Sparks referred to this fundamental change in ANC economic policy as "The Great U-Turn."[12] In 1999, when Mboweni became the country's first black Reserve Bank governor (a position he held for ten years), he reassured local and international bankers by saying: "We are not Icarus; there is no need to fear that we will fly too close to the sun." In 2000, Manuel, by then the country's first black minister of finance (a position he held for 13 years), said: "It's not a straight line from Mont Fleur to our current policy. It meanders through, but there's a fair amount in all that going back to Mont Fleur. I could close my eyes now and give you those scenarios just like *this*. I've internalized them, and if you have internalized something, then you probably carry it for life."[13]

The economic discipline of the new government enabled the annual real rate of growth of the South African economy to jump from 1 percent over 1984–1994 to 3 percent over 1994–2004. In 2010, Clem Sunter observed how well South Africa had navigated not only its transition to democracy but also the later global recession: "So take a bow, all you who were involved in the Mont Fleur initiative. You may have changed our history at a critical juncture."[14]

The Mont Fleur team's messages about the country's future were simple and compelling. Not everyone agreed with these messages: some commentators thought that the team's analysis was superficial, and many on the left thought that the conclusion about fiscal conservatism was incorrect. Nevertheless, the team succeeded in placing a crucial hypothesis and proposal about post-apartheid economic strategy on the national agenda. This proposal won the day, in part because it seemed to make sense in the context of the prevailing global economic consensus and in part because Manuel and Mboweni exercised so much influence on the economic decision making of the new government for so long. So the team's work made a difference to what happened in the country.

Mont Fleur not only contributed to but also exemplified the process through which South Africans brought about their national transformation. The essence of the Mont Fleur process— a group of leaders from across a system talking through what was happening, could happen, and needed to happen in their system, and then acting on what they learned—was employed in the hundreds of negotiating forums (most of them not using the scenario methodology as such) on every transitional issue from educational reform to urban planning to the new constitution. This was the way of working that produced the joke I had heard about the practical option and the miraculous option. South Africans succeeded in finding a way forward together. They succeeded in implementing "the miraculous option."

Neither the Mont Fleur project in particular nor the South African transition in general was perfect or complete. Many issues and actors were left out, many ideas and actions were bitterly contested, and many new dynamics and difficulties arose later on. Transforming a complex social system like South Africa is never easy or foolproof or permanent. But Mont Fleur contributed to creating peaceful forward movement in a society that was violently stuck. Rob Davies, a member of the team and later minister of trade and industry, said: "The Mont Fleur process outlined the way forward of those for us who were committed to finding a way forward."[15]

2

A New Way to Work with the Future

*W*HEN THE MONT FLEUR SCENARIO EXERCISE ended in 1992, I was left inspired and also uncertain. It was clear to me that the exercise had contributed to creating change in South Africa, but it was not clear to me whether or how this way of working could be used in other contexts. In which type of situation could transformative scenario planning be useful? To be useful, which outputs did it have to produce and which inputs did it require? And to produce these outputs, which steps were essential?

These questions set me off on an exploration that I have now been on for 20 years. After I moved to South Africa in 1993, I sought out opportunities there and elsewhere to work with people who were trying to address tough challenges. I found colleagues, and together we worked on many different projects, on different challenges, of different scales, in different countries, with different actors, using different methodologies. These experiences gave me many opportunities for trial and many opportunities for error, and so many opportunities for learning. Gradually I found answers to my questions.

When to Use Transformative Scenario Planning

The South African context that gave birth to the Mont Fleur Scenario Exercise turns out to have been a particular example of a general type of situation. Transformative scenario planning can be useful to people who find themselves in a situation that has the following three characteristics.

First, these people see the situation they are in as unacceptable, unstable, or unsustainable. Their situation may have been this way for some time, or it may be becoming this way now, or it may possibly become this way in the future. They may feel frightened or excited or confused. In any event, these people cannot or are not willing to carry on as before, or to adapt to or flee from what is happening. They think that they have no choice but to try to transform their situation. The participants in the Mont Fleur project, for example, viewed apartheid as unacceptable, unstable, and unsustainable, and saw the just-opened political negotiations as offering them an opportunity to contribute to changing it. Another, hypothetical, example might be people in a community who think that the conditions in their schools are unacceptable and want to change them.

Second, these people cannot transform their situation on their own or by working only with their friends and colleagues. Even if they want to, they are unable to impose or force through a transformation. The larger social-political-economic system (the sector or community or country) within which they and their situation are embedded is too complex—it has too many actors, too many interdependencies, too much unpredictability—to be grasped or shifted by any one person or organization or sector, even one with lots of ideas and resources and authority.[1] These people therefore need to find some way to work together with actors from across the whole system.

South Africans who wanted to transform the apartheid situation had been trying for decades to force this transformation, through mass protests, international sanctions, and armed resistance. But these efforts had not succeeded. Mont Fleur and the other multistakeholder processes of the early 1990s (which the previous forceful efforts had precipitated) provided South Africans with a new way to work with other actors from across the system. In the community example, changing the conditions in the schools might require the involvement not just of concerned citizens and school administrators but also of teachers, parents, students, and others.

Third, these people cannot transform their situation directly. The actors who need to work together to make the transformation are too polarized to be able to approach this work head-on. They agree neither on what the solution is nor even on what the problem is. At best, they agree that they face a situation they all find problematic, although in different respects and for different reasons.[2] Any attempt to implement a solution directly would therefore only increase resistance and rigidity. So the transformation must be approached indirectly, through first building shared understandings, relationships, and intentions.

The actors who came together in Mont Fleur all agreed that apartheid was irretrievably problematic and needed to be dismantled, but they came in with deep differences in their diagnoses of the ways in which it was problematic and their prescriptions for how it should be transformed. The scenario process enabled them to create common ground. In the community example, the administrators, teachers, parents, and students might have a long history of unproductive disagreements that means they cannot simply sit down and start to take action together.

Transformative scenario planning is, then, a way for people to work with complex problematic situations that they want to transform but cannot transform unilaterally or directly. This way of working with the future can be used to deal with such situations at all scales: local, sectoral, regional, national, or global. (The stories in this book are all national because this is the scale at which I have done most of my work and that I know best.)

Transformative scenario planning is not a way for actors to adapt to a situation or to force its transformation or to implement an already-formulated proposal or to negotiate between several already-formulated proposals. It is a way for actors to work cooperatively and creatively to get unstuck and to move forward.

How Transformative Scenario Planning Works

In a transformative scenario planning process, actors transform their problematic situation through transforming themselves, in four ways.

First, they transform their *understandings*. Their scenario stories articulate their collective synthesis of what is happening and could happen in and around the system of which they are part. They see their situation—and, critically important, their own roles in their situation—with fresh eyes. In a polarized or confused or stuck situation, such new, clear, shared understandings enable forward movement.

Second, the actors transform their *relationships*. Through working together in the scenario team, they enlarge their empathy for and trust in other actors on the team and across the system, and their ability and willingness to work together. This strengthening of cross-system relationships is often the most important and enduring output of such projects.

Third, the actors transform their *intentions*. Their transformed understandings and relationships shift how they see what they can and must do to deal with what is happening in their system. They transform their fundamental will.

Fourth, the actors' transformations of their understandings, relationships, and intentions enable them to transform their *actions* and thereby to transform their situation.

The story of Mont Fleur exemplifies this four-part logic. The participants constructed a new way of understanding the political, economic, and social challenges that South Africans were facing and then created four scenarios as to how South Africans could try to deal with these challenges. The participants constructed new relationships and alliances, especially between leaders of hitherto-separated parties, sectors, and races. And they constructed new intentions as to what they needed to do in their own spheres of influence to try to prevent the "Ostrich," "Lame Duck," and "Icarus" scenarios and to bring forth "Flight of the Flamingos." Over the years that followed, these new understandings, relationships, and intentions enabled the participants and others with whom they engaged to undertake a series of aligned actions that did in fact contribute to their achieving these intentions.

In the community example, a team of concerned citizens, administrators, teachers, parents, and students might construct a set of scenarios (both desirable and undesirable) about what could happen in and around their schools and community. This work together might enable them to understand and trust one another more, and to clarify what they need to do to change the conditions in their schools. Then they might be able to take action, together and separately, to effect these changes.

Transformative scenario planning can generate transformations such as those in these two examples only if three components are in place. Transformative scenario planning is a composite social technology that brings together three already-existing technologies into a new way of working that can generate new results.[3] If any one of these components is missing, this new way of working will not work.

The first component is *a whole-system team* of insightful, influential, and interested actors. These actors constitute a strategic microcosm of the system as a whole: they are not from only one part or camp or faction of the system, and they are not only observers of the system. They all want to address a particular problematic situation and know that they cannot do so alone. They choose to join this team because they think that if they can act together, then they can be more successful.

The second component is a *strong container* within which these actors can transform their understandings, relationships, and intentions.[4] The boundaries of this container are set so that the team feels enough protection and safety, as well as enough pressure and friction, to be able to do their challenging work. Building such a container requires paying attention to multiple dimensions of the space within which the team does their work: the political positioning of the exercise, so that the actors feel able to meet their counterparts from other parts of the system without being seen as having betrayed their own part; the psychosocial conditions of the work, so that the actors feel able to become aware of and challenge (and have challenged) their own thoughts and actions; and the physical locations of the meetings, so that the actors can relax and pay attention to their work without interruption or distraction.

The third component is a *rigorous process*. In a transformative scenario planning process, the actors construct a set of relevant, challenging, plausible, and clear stories about what *could* happen—not about what *will* happen (a forecast) or about what *should* happen (a wish or proposal)—and then act on what they have learned from this construction. The uniqueness of the scenario process is that it is pragmatic and inspirational, rational and intuitive, connected to and challenging of dominant understanding, and immersed in and disconnected from the complexity and conflict of the situation. Furthermore, the future is a more neutral space about which all actors are more equally ignorant.

The transformative scenario planning process that was invented at Mont Fleur originated in the adaptive scenario planning process that had been invented at Shell two decades earlier—but it turns this adaptive process on its head. In an adaptive scenario planning process, the leaders of an organization construct and employ stories about what could happen in the world outside their organization in order to formulate strategies and plans to enable their organization to fit into and survive and thrive in a range of possible futures. They use adaptive scenario planning to anticipate and adapt to futures that they think they cannot predict and cannot or should not or need not influence.

But adaptive scenario planning is useful only up to a point. Sometimes people find themselves in situations that are too unacceptable or unstable or unsustainable for them to be willing or able to go along with and adapt to. In such situations, they need an approach not simply for anticipating and adapting to the future but also for influencing or transforming it. For example, an adaptive approach to living in a crime-ridden community could involve employing locks or alarms or guards, whereas a transformative approach could involve working with others to reduce the levels of criminality. An adaptive response to climate change could involve building dikes to protect against higher sea levels, whereas a transformative approach could involve working with others to reduce emissions of greenhouse gases. Both approaches are rational, feasible, and legitimate, but they are different and require different kinds of alliances and actions.

The key difference between adaptive and transformative scenario planning is, then, one of purpose. Adaptive scenario planning uses stories about possible futures to study what could happen, whereas transformative scenario planning assumes that studying the future is insufficient, and so it also uses stories about possible futures to influence what could happen. To achieve these two different purposes, adaptive scenario planning focuses on producing new systemic understandings, whereas transformative scenario planning assumes that new understandings alone are insufficient and so also focuses on producing new cross-system relationships and new system-transforming intentions. And to produce these two different sets of outputs, adaptive scenario planning requires a rigorous process, whereas transformative scenario planning assumes that process alone is insufficient, and so it also requires a whole-system team and a strong container.

Transformative scenario planning enables people to transform their problematic situation through building a strong alliance of actors who deeply understand the situation, one another, and what they need to do.

THE FIVE STEPS OF TRANSFORMATIVE SCENARIO PLANNING

I have learned how to do transformative scenario planning through 20 years of trial and error. I have observed when these projects fail to get off the ground and when they succeed in launching, when they get stuck and when they flow, and when they collapse and when they keep on going. In this way, I have been able to discern what works and what doesn't and why, and to piece together a simple five-step process. The five steps are as follows: convening a team from across the whole system; observing what is happening; constructing stories about what could happen; discovering what can and must be done; and acting to transform the system. This process is like an old cow path: although it is not the only way forward, it is a way that has, after many alternatives were tried out over many years, proven to provide a reliable route.

These five steps can be framed as an application of the U-Process to the transformation of complex problematic situations.[5] The U-Process is a model of transformation that includes five movements: coinitiating (in transformative scenario planning, this is the convening step), cosensing (the observing and constructing steps), copresencing (the discovering step), and cocreating and coevolving (the acting step). The U-Process is an indirect process—a detour—in that it is a way to get unstuck and move forward to transform a problematic situation through pausing and stepping back from the situation. It is a creative process in that what can and must be done on the right-hand side is not visible from the left-hand side but can only be discovered only along the way. And it is a fractal process in that each step

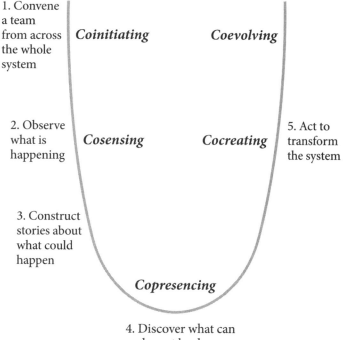

1. Convene a team from across the whole system

Coinitiating

Coevolving

2. Observe what is happening

Cosensing

Cocreating

5. Act to transform the system

3. Construct stories about what could happen

Copresencing

4. Discover what can and must be done

The Five Steps of Transformative Scenario Planning

along the U contains within it a smaller U, so that the actors repeat the five movements from coinitiating to coevolving multiple times.

Transformative scenario planning addresses problematic situations slowly and from the inside out. Over the course of the five steps, the actors gradually transform their understandings, relationships, and intentions, and thereby their actions. Through this process, the transformation ripples out from the individual leaders to the scenario team, the organizations and sectors they lead, and the larger social system.

A transformative scenario planning project can be broad or narrow, large or small, long or short. My experience suggests, however, that for a complex problematic situation to be transformed, certain ideal parameters exist. You can succeed outside of these parameters, but you will find it harder, or you will have to use methods different from the ones outlined in this book.

In the first step, a convening team of 5 to 10 people builds a whole-system scenario team of 25 to 35 leading actors (including the conveners themselves). Convening or scenario teams that are smaller than these will be unlikely to have the diversity required for whole-system insight and influence. Convening or scenario teams that are larger than these will find it difficult to develop the intimacy and engagement that the process requires. There are other methods for working with much larger teams, but these are not compatible with the structured combination of rational and intuitive processes of scenario work.

The scenario team undertakes the second, third, and fourth steps in three or four workshops of three to four days each (with supporting work being done in between the workshops), spread over four to eight months. A process with fewer workshops or workshops that are shorter or closer together will be unlikely to provide enough time for the team to go deep enough (and get lost enough) to transform their understandings, relationships, and intentions. (My partner Bill O'Brien said about the time needed for transformational work: "It takes nine months to make a baby, no matter how many people you put on the job."[6]) A process with more workshops or workshops that are longer or more spread out will find it difficult to maintain the requisite energy and momentum.

Finally, the scenario team, with others, undertakes the fifth step over another four to eight months or longer. A shorter process will be unlikely to provide enough time for the team's actions to transform their situation. But their actions could well ripple out for years, either within the scenario project or beyond its end. A transformative scenario planning project can get a process of systemic transformation started, but the process may take generations to be completed.

Transformative scenario planning is simple, but it is not easy or straightforward or guaranteed. The process is emergent; it almost never unfolds according to plan; and context-specific design and redesign are always required. So the only way to learn this process is to practice it in a variety of situations.

The five steps outlined in the following five chapters therefore constitute not so much a recipe to follow as a set of guideposts to keep in view. For each step, I give two or three diverse examples from my own experience, with a few of the examples spread across several steps. Some of the examples illustrate a team's succeeding in moving forward and some a team's failing or stopping. I focus on my own experiences, many of them in extreme situations, because these point out in bright colors the universal dynamics of these processes that are harder to discern in more ordinary situations, and they also point out from inside and up close dynamics that are harder to discern from outside and far away. I have told some of these stories before, but I use them here to draw out particular methodological lessons. Finally, for each step, I give a generalized set of process instructions. All of these processes are collated in the "Resources" chapter.

3

First Step: Convene a Team from Across the Whole System

*T*HE FIRST STEP of a transformative scenario planning project is to enroll a team of people from across a whole system who want to—and together are able to—influence the future of that system. This system can be a community, a sector, or a country: any social-political-economic whole that is too complex to be grasped or shifted by any one of its parts.

Getting the Key Actors on Board

The political, economic, and social situation in Zimbabwe has been extremely problematic. Different domestic and foreign actors have seen the situation (what is going on and why and with what consequences) entirely differently. The result has been years of polarization, violence, and stagnation.

In 2010, six Zimbabwean leaders—two businesspeople, two university vice chancellors, a labor researcher, and a church leader—decided to convene a transformative scenario process to help get their country onto a better path.[1] Each of these leaders was broadly respected, and they had a range of political histories and sympathies among them.

They thought through which sectors of Zimbabwean society—which political parties, government entities, businesses, and nongovernmental organizations—they needed to include in their process, and which individuals within each sector they would invite to form the scenario team. They talked with key leaders whose political and financial support they needed to initiate the process, including those who could stop the process if they opposed it. They named their initiative the Great Zimbabwe Scenarios Project, a reference to the remarkable 1,000-year-old monument at the site of the capital of the ancient Kingdom of Zimbabwe. They hired a project director, a facilitator, an administrator, and me.

Once the conveners had identified and invited the 40 members of the scenario team (which included the conveners themselves), two staff members conducted three-hour interviews with each participant. The staff then prepared a synthesis of the interviews, which we presented at the team's first workshop. Originally we had intended to send it out in advance of the workshop, but we were worried that it might be seen as too contentious and put people off the workshop, so we handed it out to the team members after they arrived at the venue.

The team found this report, which mirrored their own thinking in all its complexities and contradictions, riveting to read. One surprising and crucial conclusion they drew from this reading was that none of them were happy with their current situation—although they were unhappy from different perspectives and for different reasons. This report provided a solid starting point for the team's dialogue about possible futures.

One of the team members made a remark that turned out to resonate with the whole group. He said: "In Zimbabwe, we often build our houses behind high concrete walls (we call them durawalls) that prevent us from seeing anything going on outside. In our society, we do the same thing: we sit within the durawalls of our own thinking and are not aware that there might be other ways of looking at what is going on. I think that the objective of this project should be to take down our mental durawalls and enable more of us to see more of what is going on."

The team realized that to take down their durawalls, they had to suspend their assumptions. This meant that they needed to become aware of and to critically review the way each of them was thinking about what had gone on, was going on, and could go on in the country. The team continued to emphasize suspension throughout their meetings, and this helped them to work through many deep and dangerous disagreements.

The project ran into many obstacles and advanced in fits and starts. The conveners struggled to get funding (some donors thought the Zimbabwe situation was hopeless; others wanted to fund specific grassroots programs and not general multistakeholder dialogues); to overcome longstanding animosity among the actors; and to deal with the resulting organizational and administrative snags. Many times I thought the project was dead, but the conveners and staff and team members stuck with it, and the work continued.

The biggest challenge the project faced was to get all the political parties to participate in the workshops. Most politicians were suspicious of such neutral, unscripted, transpartisan encounters and confident that they could better achieve their objectives without participating. Gradually, however, over the course of the workshops, many of them came to trust the intention of the project and to see how it could be useful to the country and to themselves, and they joined the process. By the end of the project, the team was broadly representative of the key actors in the country and therefore had the potential to be broadly credible and influential. In the extremely polarized context of Zimbabwe, this in itself was an extraordinary and valuable accomplishment.

Abandoning a Convening Effort

The relationship between Aboriginal and non-Aboriginal Australians has been problematic since the British arrived in 1788. The legal status of Aboriginal people—their title to land, their right to vote, their civil liberties—has been contested continuously. Indexes of

Aboriginal health, education, incarceration, and life expectancy have consistently been much worse than those of other Australians.

Many individuals and institutions have been trying to address this problematic situation in many different ways, including job creation, social services, policy changes, lawsuits, and cultural renewal. Progress has been limited, however. The situation remains characterized by misery, hopelessness, and anger.

In October 2007, Patrick Dodson, one of the country's best-known and most respected Aboriginal leaders, proposed a national scenario dialogue. The purpose of the dialogue would be "to create a shared vision for Australia, respecting our diverse traditions, uniting us in a sense of belonging, and inspiring us to build a better future."[2] He recruited a colleague at the University of New South Wales, Sarah Maddison, and with support from me and others, they began convening this dialogue.

Our effort went through cycles of enthusiasm and hesitation. Such an ambitious initiative across such a large country required big investments of attention, time, credibility, and money. Each person who was or was to be involved (including me) therefore had to make a basic judgment as to whether this effort would work and be worth the investment. There was no way to know for sure, and so we each had to weigh a host of considerations: the value of a national scenario dialogue compared with other, more direct efforts to try to address the situation; the political context for work on this issue, including how important and urgent it was seen to be, compared with other issues; the resources available for the dialogue; and the attractiveness of working on a team with other people with unlike ideologies, interests, and personalities.

Then in December 2010, the prime minister of Australia appointed Dodson to be cochair of the Expert Panel on Constitutional Recognition of Indigenous Australians. This high-level panel offered an outstanding opportunity to change the country's basic law to address the historic injustice inflicted on Aboriginal Australians, through public consultation across the country and then the shaping of a national referendum on amending the constitution. In May

2011, in the face of this and other alternative efforts, we abandoned the scenario dialogue. Some of the people involved felt upset; others felt relieved; I felt disappointed.

Many people have tried in many ways to address the relationship of Aboriginal and non-Aboriginal Australians. Many of these initiatives have failed; ours was one. Perhaps we or others will find a more successful way to use the scenario approach—for example, with a different framing or focus or scale or timing. In working with complex problematic situations, there are no sure bets.

How to Convene a Team from Across the Whole System

You look at what is going on in your community or sector or region, and you are not content with what you see. You see possible futures that you are not willing to accept because they continue an unacceptable present, destroy an acceptable present, or fail to realize the potential of the present. And you are not willing to leave what will happen to chance or to others. You want to contribute to creating a better future.

Your concern is not about the future of everything. It is focused on some particular situation—immediate or long-term, narrow or broad, small or large—that you view as problematic and for which you feel responsibility. This situation is a state or aspect of some particular social-political-economic system. You make a judgment about the boundaries of the system you are focusing on and engaging with; you always have the option of also considering developments beyond these boundaries.

You do not need to define the situation or system precisely, and you may change your definitions as your work progresses. For example, the situation you are concerned about might initially be defined as poor health outcomes in your city. The system you are focusing on might initially be defined as the relationships among the city's citizens; health professionals; and regulatory, nonprofit, and business actors. You always have the option of also considering developments outside the city and in other fields, such as food, politics, or the economy.

You think that this system is too complex to be "fixed" from above or outside by any boss or authority. You think that you cannot change this system working only by yourself or with your friends and colleagues. It will take a team of stakeholders or actors from across the whole system: people who directly affect and are affected by what happens in the system. This team will include strangers and opponents who do not know or agree with or trust one another.

You know that there is no consensus among these actors about what should happen in the future or even about what is happening now. You think that a cross-system team could make a valuable contribution by constructing a map of possible futures to inform and inspire the actions that they and others will take. You decide to try to organize a transformative scenario planning project.

You know that such a process is too complex and demanding for any one person to be able to organize. You seek out a few allies from other parts of the system, so that together you have broader understanding and networks and credibility. Your small group is the "convening team," and from now on the "you" involved in this initiative is plural, not singular. The more fragmented and polarized the social system you are working with, the more important it is that the project be seen from the outset as nonpartisan and inclusive, and not driven by or for the benefit of only one part or faction. In the city health example, your convening team might consist of an activist, a doctor, a state official, and a businessperson, all of whom are concerned about poor health outcomes (perhaps for different reasons) and want to do something to change these outcomes.

You understand that transformative scenario planning is an emergent process, and so although you know at the outset the characteristics of the results you want to produce—understand-ings, relationships, intentions, and actions to address your prob-lematic situation—you do not know what these results will look like or how you can obtain them. You will discover these as you go. At the same time, in order to enroll others, you need to have a rough outline for what you intend to do (which you can adjust as the process unfolds). You write down the purpose of or ratio-nale for your project. You also prepare a plan for your proj-ect: its objectives, focus, participants, timeline, budget, and so on. You put in place the resources that you will need to execute your plan. For this you need to find people to make donations of money or in-kind services (for example, meeting space, trans-port, research, staff)—people who see the value of such a dialogic approach to effecting systemic change.

Such projects usually do not start with a strong, clear, com-mon purpose. They start with different people finding the sit-uation they are part of to be problematic, usually in different respects and for different reasons. These projects build shared understandings, relationships, and intentions over time.

The success of your project will depend above all on the people who will make up your scenario team. They will have the great-est influence on the content and consequences of the process, and will also be most influenced by it. Individually, the mem-bers of the team should be insightful, influential, and committed. They should be people with a stake in the future of the system (probably including young people); respected leaders of their own organizations, sectors, or communities (although they may not hold the most senior positions or even be known outside of their organizations); curious, systemic thinkers who are willing and able to reflect and speak freely and openly; and energetic and action-oriented leaders (not just spectators or followers) who will take the insights from this work and act on them in their own spheres of influence.

As a team, they should have a range of backgrounds and per-spectives (sectoral, ideological, professional, geographical, and so on, stretching beyond the usual participants in such activities to include those with different or dissenting views) that will enable them together to see the emerging system as a whole. They must also have a range of positions and connections (from business, government, and civil society) that will enable them together to influence the system as a whole. The team should be a microcosm or fractal of the whole system.

People will join this team if they think the efforts to change the system that they are undertaking on their own are or might become inadequate, and if they think joining will be worthwhile and safe. Worthwhile means that the future of the system matters to them and that working on such a heterogeneous team will enable them to have a greater (wiser, larger, faster) influence on this future. Safe means they trust that the organizers do not have a hidden or partisan agenda and that joining the team will not compromise their own interests.

The biggest challenge you will face in putting together this team is that some of the people whom you think you most need to have involved do not want to be involved. In particular, people who have a lot of power in, and who are content with, the situation as it is—who don't want it to change—will often be reluctant to join an effort that is intended to describe and open up new possible futures. (In hierarchical and authoritarian systems, it can be particularly difficult to find people who are willing to engage in new and creative thinking and acting.) You will need to search out people who are more open to such an exercise, and will also need to frame and time the exercise so that they can see it as potentially valuable rather than threatening to them. You always have the option of getting started without their being involved. In such a case, you will have to make a difficult discernment as to whether an incomplete team will be able to have the influence on the system that you are intending.

The way you identify, connect to, and enroll members of the team is simple but not easy. You talk with people, in person, one-on-one, about what you and they are trying to do. You ask them for feedback and advice (including their suggestions of about other people whom they might help you to enroll) and whether they would like to join with you. Some of the people you talk with will have no interest at all in what you are doing, others won't be interested in joining but will give you some support, and others will join you energetically. You keep going until you have a team.

While you are recruiting your whole-system team, you are also building your strong container. This means that you are setting up your project—its articulated rationale and objectives, who is leading and funding and controlling it, where it is located institutionally, how it communicates and with whom, what its ground rules are—so that the team feels both enough protection and safety and enough pressure and friction to be able to do their challenging work. You attend to the political, psychosocial, and physical dimensions of this container.

Now you conduct in-depth interviews with each team member. These interviews serve several purposes: to elicit the current thinking of the members about what is important in what is happening and might happen in and around the system, about their hopes and fears for the future of the system, and about their expectations for this project; to help them prepare for the work of the project and to respond to any confusions or concerns they might have about it; and to start to build relationships and trust among the participants.

You take careful notes in these interviews and afterward prepare a summary document that includes verbatim statements, organized by theme but without attributing specific comments to individuals. Nonattribution makes the interviews safer for the interviewee and also depersonalizes the observations. You send this document out to all the team members in advance of your first team meeting; it will enable the team to dive straight into the next step of making sense out of the rich diversity of your different perspectives on your complex context. The themes that the interviewees have emphasized and that you have highlighted in your document also serve to focus the scenario work you will be doing; they provide the touchstone for the relevance of your scenarios.

The essential challenge you face in this first step is the usual entrepreneurial challenge of trying to create something that does not yet exist. You are trying to bring together a team of leaders from across a system who don't know or understand or trust each other. The more unprecedented and difficult it is to bring together such actors, the more value you can create by doing so. The fact that these actors may never before have been brought together does not mean that they cannot be.

You have to decide, now and also later, whether to keep going in trying to organize this project. (One-half of the transformative scenario planning projects I have been involved in have failed during this first, convening step.) Many of the people you talk with are skeptical or suspicious of the initiative. Some people, who are invested in the status quo or in their own competing effort to deal with it, are hostile. You have to work hard to overcome the centrifugal fragmentation and polarization that motivated you to try to organize the project in the first place. You may need to try many times with many different people before you can find a way to get the project off the ground. You may fail and decide to walk away or to try in another way at another time.

If you have been successful with this first, convening step, you will be able to see in embryonic form the transformative outputs that such a process can produce. Through your conversations with a broad range of actors, you have gained some initial understandings of what is going on and could go on in and around the system of which you are part. A diverse group of actors, many of whom did not previously know one another, have started to form relationships with some degree of mutual comprehension and trust. And you have begun to clarify your intentions about what you can do, within and beyond this process.

4

Second Step: Observe What Is Happening

$\mathcal{T}$HE SECOND STEP of a transformative scenario planning project is for the scenario team to build up a rough shared understanding of what is happening in the system of which they are part and which they want to influence. They come to this work with differing positions in and perspectives on the system, and so this process requires them to go beyond their established views and to see with fresh eyes. It requires them to see not just their part of the system but more of the whole system. It requires them to open up and inquire and learn.

Enabling More People to See More of the Whole

From 1960 to 1996, Guatemala suffered from a genocidal civil war that tore the country's social fabric to pieces. Out of a total population of 7 million, more than 200,000 people were "disappeared" (killed) and more than 1 million were forcibly displaced. The Guatemalan state was responsible for almost all of this violence and directed almost all of it against the country's indigenous people.[1]

In 1996, the government and the insurgents signed peace accords. In 1998, a diverse group of national leaders—a university rector, an indigenous leader, a human rights activist, an ambassador to the

United Nations, a cabinet minister, two businessmen—initiated the Visión Guatemala project to help the country's people to think ahead together and so to contribute to repairing the social fabric and to implementing the accords.[2] The project was organized in cooperation with the government, funded by the United Nations Development Programme, and administered by the Association of Guatemalan Managers. The initiators chose Elena Díez Pinto to be the project director, because of her professional and personal qualifications and also because she was seen as nonpartisan (one of the initiators said that she had "neither scent nor stench") and so was credible to all sectors.

The scenario team brought together top leaders from all sectors, including politicians, clergymen, journalists, trade unionists, indigenous leaders, NGO activists, and former guerrillas and military officers. Elena Díez observed that at the beginning the team was separated into their usual camps:

> When I arrived at the hotel for lunch before the start of the initial meeting, the first thing I noticed was that the indigenous people were sitting together. The military guys were sitting together. The human rights group was sitting together. I thought, "They are not going to speak to each other." In Guatemala, we have learned to be very polite. We are so polite that we say "Yes" but think "No." I was worried that we would be so polite that the real issues would never emerge.[3]

In order to talk together productively about the future, the team first needed to create a common language for talking about the past and present. They spent their first two workshops sharing and trying to make sense of their divergent experiences and understandings. In such a divided and heterogeneous team, even the simplest encounter could be wonderfully surprising and informative. One day, I invited all the team members to choose a partner whom they thought was most different from them and for the two of them to go for a one-hour walk together in the town outside the hotel. When

they returned from their walk, some of them were literally stagger-
ing from the astonishment of having seen their common context
through such different eyes. A government official later commented:

> We are unaware of the great richness in others. We do not
> see it. There is a lot, quite a lot, to learn from people who,
> frankly speaking, we would never have considered as pos-
> sible sources of learning.[4]

Many of these encounters among the members of the scenario
team were dramatic and transformative. People from radically different backgrounds, ideologies, and worldviews—former guerrillas
and army officers, right-wing businessmen and left-wing activists,
indigenous rural leaders and members of the urban elite—talked
and worked together sincerely and openly over four three-day workshops, and this changed how many of them saw their country, each
other, and themselves. These encounters were also transformative
for me: I was moved to tears and joy by the horror and the beauty of
what was being revealed and generated.

Once I asked the team members to bring to the workshop a
physical object that for them represented the current reality of
Guatemala. We put our chairs in a circle, and one at a time they presented their objects and placed them on a low table in the middle
of the circle: a cob of corn, a staple food, and the seeds for more food,
out of which, according to indigenous legend, humanity was formed;
several pieces of traditional woven clothing, made up of many bright
colors of wool, representing the country's diverse ethnic groups; a
photo of a five-year-old daughter; two copies of the peace accords;
and a poster of Myrna Mack, an anthropologist who had been assas-
sinated for conducting research on people displaced by the war.
In this way, the team built up a rich metaphorical picture of their
diverse understandings of their complex situation.

For the second workshop, we organized a day of discussions with
panels of resource people on different topics that the team wanted
to learn more about. They were especially gripped by a panel of historians, who offered sharply contrasting interpretations of how the

country had come to be as it was. One of these historians was an indigenous professor with a doctorate, and his presence was in itself illuminating to the team; indigenous people make up half of the population of Guatemala but mostly have been marginalized.

Another time, the team traveled by bus to visit a large indigenous cooperative in the rural highlands a few hours from the workshop venue. This "learning journey" was also illuminating, showing an enterprise that was more sophisticated and successful than most of the elite from the capital city could have imagined, and providing an opportunity to have relaxed, in-depth conversations on the long bus rides.

These different structured learning experiences helped the team to build up a shared understanding of what was happening and could happen in their country. In particular, it enabled them to see the possibility of a scenario that they named "Illusion of the Moth," about a dangerous continued reliance on dictatorial leadership (like a moth buzzing around a flame); of a "Zigzag of the Beetle" scenario of erratic and uneven development; and of an unprecedented "Flight of the Fireflies" scenario of a social system constructed and illuminated by the diverse contributions of everyone. A broader view of the past and present generated a broader view of the future.

Undertaking a Disciplined Examination of Current Reality

A scenario project was initiated in Canada in 1996 in a context of rising political polarization over whether the province of Quebec should secede and so break up the country. Politicians and others had been trying to resolve this issue for decades, without success. A referendum held in Quebec the year before had rejected secession by a margin of only 1 percent. The scenario team included actors from both poles, and the name of the project—Scenarios for the Future— was carefully neutral. So was the conveners' statement about the project's purpose:

The conveners of the Scenarios for the Future Project are concerned citizens who reflect a wide range of views and interests. We have joined together for one purpose alone: to create a new opportunity to further dialogue among Canadians about the future. The conveners do not share a preference for a particular outcome of that dialogue; we have different views. But we do share the conviction that such a serious conversation, and the development of shared understandings, is essential, and urgent.[5]

The staff provided structured research support to the scenario team. During their first workshop, the team agreed on four specific subjects that they thought they needed to learn more about: new approaches to governance, including the changing relationship between the governors and the governed; the future of work and income distribution; the implications of globalization on the economy and the government, including the changing relationship between economic and political boundaries; and the implications of globalization for the emergence of a postmodern perspective, and its implications for society and for governance.

In advance of the second workshop, we found and sent to the team 15 outstanding papers on these subjects. We invited ten leading thinkers on these subjects to come to the workshop and to form four half-day panels; we called these presenters "resource persons" to emphasize that their role was to be resources for the team rather than experts imposed on it. Following each panel, the team considered the certainties and uncertainties about the future of that topic. Afterward, we prepared a 135-page transcript of the workshop, which drew out the main points raised and agreed upon without attributing any statements to particular team members. This disciplined examination of current reality laid a strong foundation for the team's later work on constructing scenarios.

Creating a Space That Enables Reperceiving

In 2008, a small group of friends and colleagues convened the Jewish-Israeli Journey project, to create common ground and common direction among the fragmented and polarized Jewish population of Israel.[6] The conveners' view was that increasingly deep divisions in this population—between left and right, religious and secular, hawks and doves, and settlers and those living within the pre-1967 borders—were making it increasingly difficult for the country to deal with its many complex challenges, including how to live in peace with Palestinians inside and outside of Israel. Ofer Zalzberg, a researcher who worked with the team, described the rationale for the effort as follows:

> The conflict has become a cacophony. As time passes, the discussion has become increasingly polarized, filled with taboos and thus simplistic. This leaves Israeli Jews with no real capacity to agree on a common strategy. . . . Mapping the key possibilities is a crucial stepping stone in moving towards an agreed strategy. A collective Jewish-Israeli focus on the plausible rather than the desired is needed.[7]

The conveners invited a diverse cross-section of Jewish-Israeli leaders to look together for answers to the question "What kind of society can we envisage, to which we and our descendants would be proud to belong and in which we could live together with our non-Jewish neighbors?" The innovation in this holistic framing was to review the stuck internal questions of Jewish values and vision in the context of the related and fraught external questions.

The divisions among Jewish Israelis and between them and their neighbors were manifested not only in growing political, intellectual, and social separation, but also in growing physical separation (for example, the "separation wall" along and inside the West Bank) and consequently shrinking shared space. So one of the important characteristics of this project was the creation of a temporary shared space, within which the members of the team were able to meet and work. This shared space was difficult to create because there were, from the beginning, many disagreements over where to meet, under what rules, and involving whom. This space felt to me like that of a difficult extended family, with a sense of connection and shared destiny as well as many long-running arguments and resentments.

The team ended up meeting in three four-day workshops, in two different locations in Israel and one in neighboring Cyprus (these different settings allowed the team to make learning journeys to different local realities). Because the team included several members of the Israeli parliament, which sat from Monday through Wednesday, the workshops took place from Thursday to Sunday and spanned the Jewish Sabbath, which lasts from Friday evening through Saturday evening. And because the team included many religious Jews, we could not do any work—any formal sessions, writing, or traveling—during this 24-hour period.

These enforced periods of nonworking turned out, to my surprise, to be the most productive of the whole process. The team used these days to relax and pray and eat and talk together. Members of the team gave thoughtful informal talks. And on each of the Saturday mornings, they gathered to study the chapter of the Torah that was prescribed for that particular week. These sessions were always friendly, argumentative, and synchronistic, with the prescribed chapter invariably raising profound questions—for example about religiosity or social divisions or neighborliness—that went to the heart of the team's scenario work.

One staff member later reflected:

> In one of our later meetings, Rabbi Azriel, from the Council of the Rabbis of the Settlements, was reflecting on how fundamentally his perspective had shifted through our working together. He said: "What I now see, and what surprises me, is that I would rather live in a scenario that I didn't choose and do not like but that takes me and my needs into consideration, than in a scenario that I do like but that does not take you into consideration." After he said that, the room fell into a sacred silence—and Israelis

Scenario	Jewish sovereignty	Jewish identity
A Jewish Home	Nation-state (territory)	Orthodox religious Zionist militarist hegemony
Two Homes for Two Peoples	Nation-state (people)	Secular Zionist statist hegemony
One Home for Two Peoples	No sovereignty	Communal (Jewish in private and public spheres but no Jewish state)
A Shared Home	Limited sovereignty	An ethnic territorial group (Jewishness equals cultural autonomy)

The Jewish-Israeli Journey Scenarios, 2008

are not often silent. This was one of those precious moments of grace that make worthwhile all of the trials and tribulations of our journey.[8]

The special space that the team created let them look at their present and their possible futures with new eyes. In particular, they were able to move beyond their separated dreams and nightmares to articulate four challenging scenarios characterized by four fundamentally different ways in which Jewish-Israeli sovereignty and identity could be understood and structured. In a context characterized by separation and stuckness, the team opened up new possibilities for how to move forward together.

How to Observe What Is Happening

You have convened your scenario team and are ready to start your work together. All of you are interested in and concerned about the future of your system, but you have radically different understandings of what needs to happen in the future, and even of what is true and important about what has happened in the past or is happening in the present. Furthermore, you cannot directly study the future, only the past and present. Science fiction writer William Gibson once said: "The future is already here—it's just not very evenly distributed."[9] So this second step of your work is to undertake a systematic and systemic study of the past and present.

Pierre Wack, the cofounder of the Shell scenario team, emphasized that the most important phase of scenario work was this "breathing in" phase of examining the current reality in all its complexity, and that this produced the foundation for the later "breathing out" phase of constructing and disseminating scenario stories. Shallow, superficial examination of current reality produces shallow, obvious scenarios about possible future realities. Wack emphasized the discipline of perception: "Seeing the future is about seeing in the right state of focus to put your finger unerringly on the key facts or insights that unlock or open understanding. Thus scenario-making is about acute perception, or better, about re-perception—becoming free of old perceptions and prejudices at the same time."[10]

You need to continue to attend to the container or space in which your team will work. The quality of your space will affect the quality of your results. In this context, space means both the physical location of your meetings—you need to find a place where you can work without distraction—and also the political, psychological, and spiritual character of the "social island" that you are creating. You need a space where the team will feel safe enough to be willing and able to relax and share and try out new ways of thinking and relating (as the Israelis did). The scenario work—what is talked about, with whom, and what conclusions are drawn—must in all cases be freely decided by the scenario team and not imposed by the organizers or funders or facilitators. So you also need to agree on ground rules that will help your team to work together creatively and productively.

The scenario process as a whole is an emergent process. So too is this observing step, and so it has a repeating rhythm of three phases: *diverging* by coming up with a lot of ideas and options; *emerging* by taking the time to think and talk these through and let them "cook"; and *converging* by drawing conclusions about what matters, what is agreed, and what to do next.[11] You need to be conscious of this three-phase movement because you need to have the openness to invite a diversity of inputs in the diverging phase; the patience to stay with the confusing and uncomfortable and creative emerging phase; and the confidence to decide and move on in the converging phase—even if not everything is settled and agreed upon (because the process is iterative, and if needed, you can come back to this observing step again later).

The *diverging phase* of this observing step involves examining what has gone on and is going on in and around your system, from as many perspectives as you are able to engage within the time and resources available. You can do this in many ways; in choosing among them, select the ones that will best enable the team to become aware of and challenge and deepen their understandings of what is happening. Your primary resources are the different perspectives, facts, and interpretations that the members of your team have as a result of their different histories and different positions in the system. To these you will add perspectives, facts, and interpretations from other people.

You can travel together to visit different parts of the system (as the Guatemalans did on their trip to the cooperative). Such a learning journey is a series of encounters, within a particular geographical area, with people or projects or places that exemplify a variety of important aspects—perhaps inspiring, perhaps sobering, perhaps intriguing—of what is going on in the larger system. The value of such encounters is that your team can have more precise and profound conversations about what is going on when you can talk not only about your different, separate experiences but also about a shared experience that you see and interpret differently.

You can invite resource people to prepare research papers or to join some of your team meetings to talk about subjects you want to learn more about (as the Canadians did). Sometimes these individuals will be expert researchers, and sometimes they will be what Pierre Wack called "remarkable persons" who have a well-grounded alternative way of looking at what is going on in the system.[12] The key to effective learning in these meetings is for the interaction to be pulled by the learners (the members of your team) rather than, as in a typical conference format, pushed by presenters.

Another way to observe what is going on in your system is to observe yourselves (as the Israelis did). If your team is to some extent a microcosm of the social system you are trying to understand and influence, and if you are willing to pay attention to and talk about what is happening within and among yourselves— events and patterns, thoughts and feelings—then you have the opportunity to observe in your own meeting room some of the important dynamics present in the larger system.

The *emerging phase* of this sense-making step involves taking the time, individually and together, to sit with your many observations and try to make sense of what is going on in the system. In doing this, it is important that you not only share your observations verbally or in handed-out papers but also make and keep your observations visible to the whole team. You can do this by writing or drawing on flip charts or sticky notes, or by constructing physical models with everyday objects or modeling bricks.[13] These tangible representations of your thinking help you to collectively make sense of what you are observing, by looking at it, organizing it, disaggregating and aggregating it, revising it, and so on.

One way you can make sense of your observations is by searching for driving forces. A driving force is a social, technological, economic, environmental, cultural, or political force in or around the system, a small change in which would have a big impact on those aspects of the system that matter to you. You can look at these driving forces at three levels: at the level of observable events (like newspaper headlines), at the level of repeating patterns of events across time or space, and at the level of systemic structures (relationships between different parts of the system, the distributions of resources and power, the rules and habits and ways of thinking, and so on).[14] An example of a driving force would be "the level of political attention being paid to environmental challenges" (a small change in which would have a big impact on what happens to technology and energy and business). At the level of events, this driving force could manifest as a regulatory decision in favor of or opposed to a particular power plant; at the level of patterns, as a series of such regulatory decisions; and at the level of structure, as new laws or campaigning organizations or consumption habits.

You are not trying to build a complete model of what is happening in and around the system: that would not be possible. You are trying to systematize and deepen your team's conversation about what is happening, and in particular to include not only observations about events and patterns but also hypotheses about underlying structures. The greater your capacity to see systems at the level of structures, the greater your capacity to understand and influence these systems.

The *converging phase* of this sense-making step draws conclusions about what is going on in the system in the present that matters most for the future. These conclusions can be tentative: you may iterate several times between this observing step and the next, constructing one. One kind of conclusion that is particularly useful for constructing scenarios is two lists, of certainties and uncertainties. You ask: Looking at the level of systemic structure at the forces driving our system, what are the most important certainties about the future? And what are the most important uncertainties about the future, and what are two possible poles of each uncertainty? These certainties will, by definition, be present in all scenarios, while the uncertainties will be the primary differentiators between scenarios. In the previous example, a certainty might be increasing public awareness of environmental challenges. An uncertainty might be the relative political prioritization of environmental versus economic concerns, and the two poles of this might be the assigning of higher priority to environmental concerns than to economic ones, and vice versa.

Just as you cannot build a complete model of the current reality of the whole system, you also cannot definitively calculate certainties and uncertainties about the future. All you can do is reach agreement in the team about certainties and uncertainties, through disciplined and open observation of current reality and through systematic and patient examination of underlying systemic structures.

During this second, observing step and then the third, constructing one, you must keep your focus on what *could* happen and not on what you want to happen. One of the dilemmas of transformative (as opposed to adaptive) scenario planning is that you are motivated to do this work because you passionately want to contribute to creating better futures, and at the same time the work requires that you dispassionately examine a range of possible futures, including ones that you might consider better and ones you might consider worse. You deal with this dilemma by decoupling and alternating between these passionate and dispassionate stances—and during these two steps you must hold the dispassionate one. This means that you delay or at least contain conversations about what it is about what is going on or could go on that you want or don't want, like or don't like, or think is good or bad. Such judgments cloud these observing and constructing steps. Only in the fourth, discovering step will you come back to your passionate, normative evaluations.

By the end of this observing step, then, you have further built up your transformative outputs. You have rich shared understandings, with more of you seeing more of the whole of the system of which you are all part. Your cross-system relationships have deepened from the experience of thoughtfully exploring complex and contentious terrain together, and from clarifying where you agree and disagree. And you are starting to develop a common intention about what is going on in the system that requires your attention and energy.

5

Third Step: Construct Stories about What Could Happen

HE THIRD STEP of a transformative scenario planning project is for the team to construct a useful set of scenarios about what could happen in and around their system. To be useful, the scenarios must be relevant, challenging, plausible, and clear. Useful scenarios open up and enable movement in the thinking and acting of actors across the system.

Using the Deductive Method to Generate Four Scenarios from Two Key Uncertainties

The Great Zimbabwe Scenarios team deepened their shared understanding of certainties and uncertainties about the future by talking through their country's history, the perspectives of invited resource persons, and their own experiences. By their third workshop, held at a hotel next to the Great Zimbabwe monument, they were focusing on two key uncertainties that they thought were essential to understanding the future.

The first key uncertainty was whether the people of Zimbabwe would experience poverty or well-being. The second was whether leaders at different levels in Zimbabwe would connect, engage, and resonate with the people and create cohesion among different groups, and thereby generate collective energy toward attaining

51

societal goals. The team connected this second uncertainty to their most painful, contentious, and crucial questions about political and social diversity and inclusion. The team also thought that they could, if they worked with others, influence the outcome of this second uncertainty and therefore help determine which scenario would be more likely to occur.

Several powerful new participants from political parties and the security sector joined the team at this third workshop. On the first day, their joining created contention and tension; that night I slept badly. But by the middle of the second day, the whole group came together into a relaxed and creative flow; I was relieved. That afternoon, we all walked through the site of Great Zimbabwe and returned to the meeting room subdued and reflective. Three of the participants commented: "The fact that we can all stand in awe of an incredible architecture of someone who dared to believe in themselves and to create something out of nothing implies that if we dare to believe in ourselves, not doubt ourselves, then future generations can also stand in awe and salute us." ... "The monument spoke to me of leadership, vision, staying power, and self-sufficiency. If we have that solid leadership, we can do anything." ... "For me the lessons came from choosing whom to walk with: choosing to walk with someone I don't usually walk with, but knowing we have the same destination, to a place of greatness. Building this nation is going to take a willingness to build relationships across bridges—cultural, racial, political—taking us out of our comfort zones and stepping into different conversations than we are used to. This suspension has been the greatest gift: to transcend such differences so as to have one conversation."[1]

Over the course of this workshop, the team agreed on the content of the four scenarios that they deduced from their two key uncertainties. They then chose names for the scenarios, considering and rejecting several sets of names with consistent themes (such as animal names) and instead choosing a set with a mixture of themes—a national trait, a machine, two animals—to evoke the radically different characteristics of the different scenarios. In the weeks that followed, they wrote up these scenarios, incorporating the metaphor of each and exploring the particular challenge posed by each:

- "The Stone People" depicts a government that is responsive to the needs of citizens and that successfully addresses the social, economic, and political concerns that have historically shaped the nation. The Great Zimbabwe Monument is a remarkable work of architecture; built with beautifully cut stone bricks, it holds together without mortar, testifying to exceptional skill and innovation. It has retained its character through decades of gentle rain, sweet sunshine, occasional storms, and raging sun. Though in some places some of the walls are starting to collapse, it is not a ruin. The major challenge of this scenario is for national leaders to put aside their differences and out of shared national values and vision build one nation where all can belong.
- "Stimela" (the Ndebele word for "locomotive") depicts a leadership that provides a viable developmental vision, rallies the nation behind it, and successfully implements this vision according to an agreed-upon development plan. The locomotive is a critical mode of transport that lubricates industries and economies; she follows a route that is well known and defined; she does not create new roads but simply follows the cold steel tracks bringing goods and passengers to their desired destination; there are no surprise detours. The major challenge of this scenario is that this directed approach to development may cause the people to disengage from the leadership.
- "The Vulture State" depicts a government that fails to connect with its people and that pursues a national development agenda that benefits only a few. Vultures scavenge areas where carcasses are available for their sustenance; they have a knack for identifying weak prey that affords them a bountiful meal; they are scared off if the prey puts up a fight but never fly too far away; they have no qualms about eating their prey alive. The major challenge in this scenario is for leaders to focus on national development and be willing to detach from their personal economic interests.

- "The Chameleon" depicts a coalition government that struggles to move the nation forward, as politicians remain politically connected to their own partisan and ideological policy positions. The slow-moving chameleon first combats threats by disguising itself with the color of its terrain. It can post good speeds if chasing prey or in danger. Yet it can fail to respond to danger and be caught flat-footed. Its true colors can often be forgotten because it consistently blends with its surroundings. The major challenge in this scenario is for an inclusive system of governance to be able to create development pathways that effectively manage diversity in order to build one nation.

In the midst of the high levels of polarization and conflict in Zimbabwe, these scenarios represent a significant convergence across all sectors on a way of thinking about the choices and challenges that the country faces.

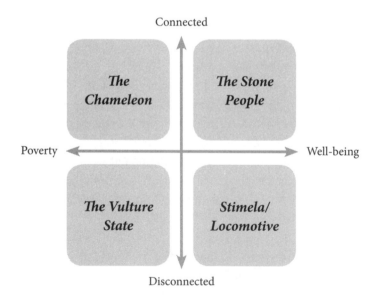

The Great Zimbabwe Scenarios, 2012

Using the Inductive Method to Generate
Out-of-the-Box Scenarios

In 2009, the North and South of Sudan—combined, the largest country in Africa, sharing borders with nine countries—seemed on the brink of returning to the civil war that between 1983 and 2005 had killed two million people and displaced four million more. That war had ended with the signing of the Comprehensive Peace Agreement, which called for a referendum to be held in 2011 on the secession of South Sudan. But now conflict was escalating, and many local and international observers were worried that the agreement might be breached and the situation might unravel and plunge the whole region into violence.

The Institute for Security Studies, a think tank based in South Africa, organized a transformative scenario planning project.[2] They invited top leaders from both the National Congress Party (NCP) and the Sudan People's Liberation Movement (SPLM), the ruling parties in the North and South, respectively, plus other national and international actors to participate in a single four-day workshop in Pretoria. The invitees understood that stepping away from their highly pressured normal context could be useful and agreed to come to the workshop. Pagan Amum, the secretary general of the SPLM, said to me before the workshop: "I was in the war in the bush, and I know that it is possible to be faced with a course of action that you realize will produce disastrous results, but in the pressure of the situation to take that course of action nevertheless. I want my colleagues to have the opportunity to pause and step back and think through carefully what they are doing."

Several international think tanks had already produced scenarios for Sudan that started from the two obvious uncertainties about the future (Will South Sudan secede? Will North and South Sudan return to civil war?) and explored the four obvious scenarios that could be deduced from these uncertainties (war and secession, peace and secession, war and unity, peace and unity). In this workshop, we wanted to think outside of this box, and so we used a different method to construct scenarios. The team brainstormed 30 candidate scenarios, including scenarios that embodied the conventional wisdom of the different parties about what would or should happen. From these 30, they succeeded, after a long and complicated conversation, in choosing four that they thought would be most useful to improving the quality of strategic thinking among themselves and their colleagues about the future of Sudan.

The four scenarios they chose included two of the familiar ones and two others that were new. There was a scenario of peaceful coexistence, "The Final Dawning," and one of total war, "A Sun That Never Rises." Then there was a scenario, "Muddling Through," of years of ambiguous accommodation with neither clear war nor clear peace, for which none of the actors were prepared. And there was a scenario, "Bypass," of an emergency circumvention of the Comprehensive Peace Agreement to prevent a return to war; this was a heretical option for all the actors who had been focusing for years on the difficult implementation of the agreement.

I was surprised and impressed with the rationality with which the participants approached their task of building scenarios about such life-and-death matters. As Amum had hoped, most of the participants wanted to think through carefully what could happen and what they could do about it. I remember leaning over a table of Northern participants, coaching them through an evaluation of the opportunities and threats they would face if the bloody "A Sun That Never Rises" scenario were to occur.

The team's nonobvious scenarios enabled them to reach nonobvious conclusions. One was that the parties needed to focus their energies not only on the implementation of the agreement but also on maintaining relationships among themselves in order to be able to resolve the dangerous conflicts that would inevitably continue to arise, even after a referendum. Mustafa Osman, presidential adviser of the NCP, later wrote: "There were not many differences among all the parties at that workshop, but it is that small percentage of what makes us different that has been enhanced in the past. We now need to focus on our commonalities."[3]

In July 2011, South Sudan seceded peacefully. Later, fighting broke out along the North-South border. The future of Sudan remains both unpredictable and influenceable.

How to Construct Stories about What Could Happen

Now that your team has built a rich shared understanding of what is happening in and around your system—your community, sector, country, or region—you are ready to construct scenarios. Your objective is to find, among the infinite number of possible stories about what could happen, the two or three or four stories that you think would be most useful. (Fewer than two stories would be a forecast or a vision, not scenarios; more than four would be too many to remember, communicate, and use.) Scenarios are useful when they meet four criteria: they must be *relevant*, illuminating current circumstances and concerns, and connected to current thinking; *challenging*, making important dynamics that are invisible visible and raising questions about current thinking; *plausible*, logical and fact based; and *clear*, accessible, memorable, and distinct from one another.

There are two common methods for moving from the lists of certainties and uncertainties that you produced in your previous, observing step to a set of scenarios.[4] The certainties will, by definition, take on the same value in all the scenarios. The uncertainties, in contrast, will take on different values in different scenarios.

The first, *deductive* method (the one the Zimbabweans used) starts by choosing two key uncertainties. These are the ones that, relative to the other uncertainties, both have the greatest impact on the system and are the most unpredictable. Furthermore, one or both of these two key uncertainties should have outcomes that you—alone or with your team or with others—can influence.[5]

Uncertainties that meet all three of these criteria will give you scenarios that are useful in that they provoke questions about what actions you must take both to adapt to the future and also to influence it.

You use the two uncertainties you have chosen as the two axes of a two-by-two matrix, yielding four scenarios. Sometimes one or two of the quadrants are implausible, and so you end up with fewer scenarios. You may need to try out several pairs of key uncertainties until you find a pair that produces scenarios that are useful.

With the second, *inductive* method (the one that the Sudanese used), you start by brainstorming many possible scenarios; then you group and iterate these, and you choose from among them the two or three or four most useful ones. The inductive method is a form of the "intuitive logics" approach developed at Shell, which draws on a team's collective intuition about what could happen.[6]

Neither of these methods is mechanical; both require you to make a judgment about which of the many possible stories are the most useful ones. In the deductive method, you make the critical judgment early when you choose two key uncertainties; whereas in the inductive method, you make the critical judgment later when you choose among the many possible scenarios. In the deductive method, first you develop the structure of the set of scenarios, and then you develop the structure of each scenario; whereas in the inductive method, you do the opposite. The main advantage of the deductive method is that it is more straightforward, whereas the main advantage of the inductive one is that it is more creative. In all cases your point of reference must be the four criteria: which, of the many possible stories, are the two or three or four that are most relevant, challenging, plausible, and clear?

Once you have decided on this skeleton set of useful scenarios, you must put flesh on the bones. This means that you must elaborate each scenario so that it consists not simply of a few general descriptors but of a specific logical narrative: in this scenario, what happens and why, through what series of hypothetical future events (this event leads to that event, which results in another event, and so on), and with what consequences. You choose names for the scenarios that accurately capture the essence of each story and will also challenge and open up the thinking of the actors you are trying to inform and influence.

You also need to come up with at least one picture that depicts all of your scenarios and shows how they relate to one another. This picture can take many forms, including a logic tree (as in the Mont Fleur example in chapter 1), a table comparing the scenarios across several key uncertainties (the Jewish-Israeli example in chapter 4), a graph showing the paths of each scenario from the present into the future (the Dinokeng example in chapter 6), a matrix formed by the outcomes of two key uncertainties (the Great Zimbabwe example in chapter 5 and the Scenarios for the Future example in chapter 6), or a set of evocative images (the Destino Colombia example in chapter 8).

Finally, you document the scenarios in a way that will enable you to communicate your work compellingly. You can do this using different media: a brief or extended report, an illustrative quantification of the stories, a scripted presentation, a video, a cartoon, and/or a play. Part of the power of scenarios is that they are stories and as such can evoke thought and emotion and action. The power of transformative scenarios, in particular, is that they are stories about the actors in the system that you are part of and about the choices they make and the consequences of these choices. You need to communicate your scenarios so that they tap into this power.

Your scenarios provide a rigorous and penetrating description of what is happening and could happen in and around your system. They highlight the opportunities and threats and choices that you and others face. Now you are ready to use these scenarios to decide how to move forward.

6

Fourth Step: Discover What Can and Must Be Done

*T*HE FOURTH STEP of a transformative scenario planning project is for the team to see what their scenarios tell them about what they can and must do. These conclusions may be about actions that they need to take to adapt to things they cannot influence, or about actions to influence things they can. These conclusions may be about actions that they need to take jointly or separately. In this step, the team crystallizes their intentions.

Clarifying What to Do Together and Separately

In 2008, Old Mutual, the financial services group that had sponsored one of the South African scenario projects that preceded Mont Fleur, initiated a new project: the Dinokeng Scenarios.[1] (*Dinokeng* is a Sepedi word meaning "place of rivers" and was the name of the location of the project's workshops.) Many South Africans were confused and concerned about what was going on in their country: the African National Congress, which had been in power since the 1994 democratic election, was roiled by factional battles; the economy was weak, in part because of chronic power shortages; and the public education, health, and safety systems were in crisis. People were keen to talk with one another to understand what was going on and to find ways to contribute to getting the national transformation back on track. Almost all the leaders who were invited to join the scenario team accepted immediately.

After ten days of working together, the team agreed on three scenarios. These were "Walk Apart," a story of continued social disintegration and decay; "Walk Behind," a story of an interventionist and paternalistic state; and "Walk Together," a story of an enabling state and an engaged citizenry. The team all agreed that a healthy future for the country depended on citizens and leaders from all sectors (not just the government) reengaging actively and robustly with the country's tough challenges—as many had done during the pre-1994 fight against apartheid but as most had not after 1994. This was the main message that they focused on when they later disseminated their scenarios, and it was the main message that was taken up in

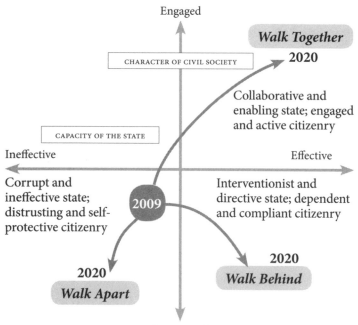

The Dinokeng Scenarios, South Africa, 2009

how South Africans thought about their situation and about what they needed to do about it.

The team did not all agree, however, that "Walk Behind" would necessarily produce results inferior to "Walk Together." The differences between these scenarios crystallized a critical debate among South Africans about the role that the state should play in national development. The team also did not agree on whether they needed to choose one of the scenarios as the one they wanted—as their vision or proposal. In their own organizations and spheres of influence, the members of the team therefore pursued some courses of action that were aligned and some that were divergent.

The members of the Dinokeng team had expanded their shared understanding of their situation and of their roles in it. The remaining misalignment among them was neither unusual nor problematic. This ideologically and politically heterogeneous group had simply reached the limit of what they thought they needed and were willing to agree on. Every group has such a limit; complete alignment is not necessary or even desirable. What is important is that the team is able to help their system to get unstuck and move forward. The Dinokeng team accomplished this.

Scenarios That Fail to Generate Action

The Canadian Scenarios for the Future team struggled to agree on a set of scenarios that they considered both plausible and challenging. Many of the members of the team were comfortable with the way things were going in the country and with their existing stories about what was happening and could happen, and they were cautious and critical (even cynical) about new stories. The staff managed the process politely, carefully, and tightly. So the work went slowly and haltingly, and we ended up needing to add an extra, fifth workshop. Our extremely cautious approach meant that the process never got into flow.

The team ended up framing their scenarios in terms of two key uncertainties about what might happen in the future: "Will our society and economy adapt quickly or slowly to global change, and will our governing systems change through evolution or by making a sharp break with the past?"[2] ("A sharp break" was a reference to the sensitive question of Quebec secession.) The four possible combinations of these two uncertainties corresponded to four scenarios, which the team named using arch-Canadian canoeing metaphors:

- "Drift," in which governing systems evolve incrementally, and the society and economy adapt less adequately and too slowly to change
- "Capsize," in which an unsuccessful sharp break reinforces and is reinforced by a slow, inadequate adaptation by the society and economy to a changing world
- "Shoot the Rapids," in which a sharp break successfully resolves the long-standing constitutional impasse as part of a quick, effective adaptation by the society and economy to global change
- "Portage," in which individuals, communities, business, and labor work together to adapt effectively to a changing world, with governing systems evolving to support this adaptation

How our governance system changes

		Sharp break	Evolution
How our society and economy adapt to a changing world	Quickly	*Shoot the Rapids*	*Portage*
	Slowly	*Capsize*	*Drift*

Scenarios for the Future, Canada, 1998

From these scenarios the team inferred the following: "Our world is changing rapidly and fundamentally. How quickly and effectively our society and economy adapt to these changes is more crucial to our future than whether our governing systems change through evolution or a sharp break with the past." This conclusion was timid and un-challenging. Soon afterward, the project ran out of energy and money. The scenarios were presented at one national conference but were (to my knowledge) never used again.

At the beginning of the first workshop, one of the organizers had expressed his greatest fear about the project. It was "that we stay within the usual conversation, repeat things we have said often before, and play out our usual roles." His fear was realized.

How to Discover What Can and Must Be Done

You have constructed a set of scenarios about what could happen in and around your system. Your objective in undertaking this process was not to construct scenarios as an end in themselves but to use them to transform your system. So now you step back and see what meanings and conclusions you can draw from your scenarios about what you can and must do. These are conclusions about what options you have and what actions you intend to take, to achieve what objectives, with what allies.

From the perspective of the project process, stepping back corresponds to the copresencing movement at the bottom of the U. Many times during the process so far, you have paused, quieted down, and reflected on what was at that moment going on in yourself, in your team, and in your system. This pausing in the middle of the work provides a simple and useful interruption in the pressured busyness of an intellectually, emotionally, and politically demanding process. It helps you to notice what is going on, what it means, and what you need to do next. You can pause for a few seconds of self-awareness or a few minutes of quiet reflection or journaling in the group. Or you can pause for lon-ger: a few hours in silence in nature (without books or cell phones or other distractions), as part of one of your workshops, or even a few days of silent retreat. You will find that all of these pattern-interrupting practices are surprisingly creative and productive.

The way you pause follows your usual diverging-emerging-converging rhythm. You reflect individually; then you share your reflections in the team; and then you make sense of these reflec-tions. Now, in this fourth, discovering step, you apply this same practice to reflecting on the meaning of the scenarios for what you can and must do. You may discover this meaning quickly, in a single team conversation, or it may come slowly, after you have mulled over the scenarios for months. It may be obvious to all of you, or it may be the subject of a lot of debate and dialogue.

From the perspective of the project content, you can draw two kinds of meanings or conclusions from your scenar-ios. These correspond to the two complementary stances that Reinhold Niebuhr identified in his maxim: "Lord grant me the serenity to accept the things I cannot change, the courage to change the things I can, and the wisdom to know the differ-ence." The first, the *adaptive* stance, assumes that you cannot change the system you are part of and implies that you must accept it and adapt to it serenely. The second, the *transforma-tive* stance, assumes that you *can* change the system (in most cases through allying with others) and implies that you must try to do so courageously.

In transformative scenario planning, you employ both of these stances. The transformative assumption is what moti-vated your transformative scenario planning effort. But the adaptive assumption is also vital because it helps you to avoid the hubristic error of overestimating your influence on the sys-tem and so being caught dangerously unprepared when the future unfolds in a way that you hoped or wished it wouldn't. You need the wisdom to know which aspects of your situa-tion demand which stance: which combination of adaptive and transformative actions you need to take in your specific context. This wisdom may emerge only gradually over the course of your scenario work, as you come to see and grasp the adaptive and transformative meanings and implications of your scenarios.

First you take the adaptive stance. You look at your scenarios of possible futures, any of which could plausibly occur—whether or not you like them or want them. One scenario at a time, you ask: if this scenario occurred, what would I or my organization or community or country have to do to survive and thrive? For this exercise, a reverse-order "SWOT" analysis can be useful: *if* this scenario occurred, which *opportunities* and *threats* would we face, and which of our *strengths* and *weaknesses* would be important? For example, if the "Walk Behind" scenario occurred, then as a businessperson I would face the threat of increased government intervention, and my lack of connections to the government would be a weakness, so in order to adapt to this future, I would need to find business partners with good connections to the government.

Next you take the transformative stance. You look at your scenarios as a set and ask: Which futures are better for me and my organization or community or country? Which futures do I want, and which do I not want? The 1960s slogan "If you're not part of the solution, you're part of the problem" misses the crucial point, which is that if you're not part of the problem, you can't be part of the solution.[3] In other words, if you can't see the ways in which what you are doing or not doing is contributing to what is happening in the present, then you can't contribute to what could happen in the future—except from outside or above the system, by pushing. So the fundamental transformative questions are: What is my role in what is happening and could happen? What is my responsibility? What does the future need of me? For example, I might think that "Walk Together" would be better for my business and for the country but be concerned that the distance that I and other businesspeople are taking from the government is encouraging politicians to push for "Walk Behind," and so I need to proactively build alliances with political as well as civil society actors.

As you cycle and iterate between these two complementary stances, you will gradually discover the meaning that the scenarios have for you. In doing this, you are gradually discovering the intersection of the answers to the two fundamental and complementary questions that underlie all strategic thinking: What is happening in the world that could have an impact on us? And what impact do we want to have on the world?

Out of all this, you draw conclusions about what you must do. Some of your conclusions and actions will be congruent across your team, and you will want to work on these together; others will be congruent across your team, and you will want to work on them in alignment but separately; and others will differ across your team—perhaps even be in opposition—and on these you will part ways. All these responses are legitimate and can be useful in getting unstuck and moving forward on addressing your problematic situation. From the examples of conclusions given above, we might decide to discuss the dangers of "Walk Behind" with the government and other actors; we might build our own local alliances separately; and we might compete for well-connected business partners.

Now you can taste the fruits of your scenario work. You have reached important understandings about the implications of the scenarios. Your relationships have strengthened through doing intellectually and politically and personally demanding work together. And you have crystallized your intentions: you know what to do.

7

Fifth Step: Act to Transform the System

_J_N THE FIFTH AND FINAL STEP of a transformative scenario planning project, the members of the team act, with one another and with others from across the system, to transform their problematic situation. These actions can take any number of forms: campaigns, meetings, movements, publications, projects, policies, initiatives, institutions, or legislation; private or public; short-term or long-term. The activities of this step, more than those of the previous steps, will therefore generally not be able to be foreseen or planned in advance. These activities will furthermore not necessarily be organized by or seen as part of the scenario project as such.

The understandings, relationships, intentions, and actions that the scenario process produced are seeds. Sometimes they fail to germinate, and sometimes they fall on hard or barren soil. Even when they do sprout, they don't necessarily grow in ways that can be predicted or controlled. So this fifth step, even more than the previous ones, is emergent. The team needs to pay attention to where and how its work is taking root and to cultivate these new possibilities.

Contributing a New and Powerful Framing

The objective of the Dinokeng Scenarios that was originally articulated by the project's conveners was to create "a space and language for open, reflective, and reasoned strategic conversation among South Africans about possible futures for the country and the opportunities, risks, and choices these futures present." The importance of achieving this objective was reinforced by the primary conclusion that the team drew from their scenarios: that citizens' reengaging in shaping the future of the country was a vital and perhaps essential condition for a good future.

The team took on seriously the task of creating a space and language in which citizens could talk through the scenarios and in this way reengage with the future. In the months before we launched our report publicly, we held private briefings with more than 30 national leaders, including the president. The launch of our report, in May 2009 (right after a national election but before the new government took office), got full pages of coverage in all the major newspapers. Over the two years after the launch, we distributed 20,000 copies of our full 80-page report, 10,000 copies (in five languages) of a 32-page summary report, and 2,000 copies of a 30-minute video; we ran more than 100 workshops for political, business, nongovernmental, and community organizations in every province and every major city; we created five weekly inserts in a national chain of newspapers (with 2 million readers) and six weekly televised debates (with 500,000 viewers); our work was the subject of more than 150 newspaper articles and more than 25 radio and television broadcasts; and our website had 40,000 hits. So we succeeded in placing the simple, crucial "Walk Together" insight about citizen reengagement, along with the question about the role of the "Walk Behind" developmental state, into the center of South African discourse about the future.

This Dinokeng thinking has reverberated in the national discourse. One important example is the plan for the country prepared by the National Planning Commission. This new body was set up in 2010 by the government and is composed of 26 of the country's most respected leaders from different sectors, including two people who were members of the Dinokeng team and three of the Mont Fleur team. Cabinet minister Trevor Manuel, the chairperson of the commission, summarized the essence of the plan as follows:

> I want to talk about what the National Planning Commission believes is necessary to drive the changes that we owe ourselves and the next generations of South Africans. Essentially we argue that an active state (whether this is real or imagined) and a passive citizenry will create more of [the unsatisfactory situation that] we now live through. So the biggest changes we propose are in the area of how society functions. Firstly, we are arguing for active citizenry in every aspect of society—be this in respect to schools, fighting crime, overseeing health care, requiring reports from and giving mandates to the three spheres of government—in all of this we need to work to ensure that citizens are actively engaged. The second feature of the change is to promote the voice of leadership throughout every aspect of society. The third focus area is on a capable state. These three aspects are dynamically linked and together determine the outcome.[1]

Vincent Maphai is an intellectual and businessman who was a convener of both Mont Fleur and Dinokeng and is now a member of the commission. He said:

> The biggest contribution we made with Dinokeng was changing the mindset and forcing people to take responsibility. That has been the powerful message, and not a particularly pleasant message to give to a society that is waiting for Mandela to give them things. We were bold there. I don't believe that you can influence people overnight, but you can plant a seed and, like the story of soil in the Bible, it depends on where the seed ultimately falls. Our job is to disseminate.[2]

Several members of the Dinokeng team, as well as other people inspired by the work, have established new citizens' movements to implement the "Walk Together" scenario. These movements are focused on the crucial problematic situations of education and employment, and they emphasize the necessity of building up active citizen involvement on these and other challenges. Mamphela Ramphele, a prominent activist, academic, and businesswoman who was the chairperson of the Dinokeng conveners, has been deeply involved in many of these initiatives and explains why she thinks they are necessary:

> No democracy anywhere in the world has ever managed to be consolidated without the active engagement of civil society and individual citizens....The failure of South Africans to embrace the Dinokeng Scenarios in 2009 was a source of great frustration for me. But it was largely due to the fact that we didn't understand, as the conveners of those scenarios, just how deeply wounded South Africans were. We expected disengaged South Africans to simply realize the errors of their ways and choose to walk together. The walking apart and walking behind are symptoms of a wounded society. Unless we confront this woundedness, we cannot make progress.[3]

The large-scale dissemination of the Dinokeng scenarios was intended to regenerate active participation by South Africans in building their new democracy, and it has begun to do so. In this way, the scenarios have helped to open up and strengthen the country's politics and its capacity to deal with its challenges.

Multiplying a New Way of Working
The Visión Guatemala project, launched just after the signing of the accords that ended the long, genocidal civil war, built a team of leaders from across the whole society with strong understandings, relationships, and intentions. Outside of the formal boundaries of the

project while it was ongoing, and then for many years after the project ended, the members of the team built on these results as they took actions in their own organizations and spheres of influence. Sometimes they took these actions separately and sometimes they did so in alliance with other team members. Their continued cooperation was facilitated by Elena Díez, the executive director of Visión Guatemala, who after the end of the project continued to play prominent roles in various important Guatemalan and Latin American societal transformation organizations.

Lars Franklin, the United Nations' representative in Guatemala, said that the impact of Visión Guatemala could best be understood by looking at the many seeds that the project planted and nurtured.[4] These included four presidential candidates and campaigns; contributions to the Commission for Historical Clarification, the Fiscal Agreement Commission, and the Peace Accords Monitoring Commission; work on municipal development strategies, a national antipoverty strategy, and a new university curriculum; and six spinoff national dialogue processes.

Lizardo Sosa, the president of the Guatemalan Central Bank, commented on the subtle way that the project influenced what was happening in the country:

> I don't know how much of what happened later in the country has to do with Visión Guatemala. I will mention one project in which I participated: to get the process of making a fiscal agreement going. If you look at the actors who were involved in this and similar efforts, there are people who have been in Visión Guatemala. I don't know how much of what each one of us experienced in the Visión Guatemala process has contributed to the little or lot we have advanced on this subject, which I believe is a lot. One would also have to observe that its presence in other spheres, like salt in the world, is already impregnated in the way of being and behaving of some groups. But it is difficult to assess, because Visión Guatemala is almost like the Apostles to whom Christ said: "Take up

your cross and follow me." Yes, it is like that: not through writing or radio or television, but through a process of inner reflection.[5]

Gonzalo de Villa, a university rector, suggested that the scenarios were only the means for the team and others to accomplish the larger end of finding new ways to work together to build their country. He said:

What place to assign to the construction of scenarios as such? It is good that they were made, but that was not necessarily what was most important. The story of the scenarios is like the story anthropologist Bronislaw Malinowski tells of a system he discovered in some South Sea islands. He found that an extremely sophisticated mechanism exists by which people from some islands travel to others and make exchanges of seashells. From the point of view of economic logic, this makes no sense at all: to risk lives in very long voyages to exchange shells. But in the end, he discovers that the shells are the great pretext to do another whole bunch of things that are the ones that really matter. I believe that the scenarios are the shells of Visión Guatemala. They were the great pretext to do what we needed to do.[6]

In the years since Visión Guatemala, the country has continued to struggle with severe challenges. The optimism engendered by the signing of the peace accords has dissipated; the government of President Álvaro Colom (a member of Visión Guatemala) ran into many problems; the new government of President Otto Pérez Molina, a former army general, has awakened hopes of increased security and fears of a return to militarism. Through all this, the legacy of Visión Guatemala is the cross-system relationships and the knowledge that it is possible to work together to create better futures.

How to Act to Transform the System

You have brought together a whole-system team of actors, you have constructed scenarios about what could happen in and around the system you are all part of, and you have reached conclusions about what you will do to deal with the opportunities and challenges posed by these scenarios.

You have now turned the corner of the U of the transformative scenario planning process. One key characteristic of the process up to now has been that as a team you have not taken any action beyond your private work of constructing scenarios. This disciplined detachment and neutrality has helped you to step back and see with fresh eyes what is happening and could happen, and what you can and must do about it.

Now the time has come for the scenario team to engage in public action. You can do this in a range of ways. On one end of the spectrum, some or all of the members of your team can, together with others whom you recruit to join you, work on executing a joint plan based on the understandings, relationships, and intentions that you have generated through your work. At the other end of the spectrum, the members of your team can act separately, in alignment with one another or not, in their own spheres of influence—organization, network, or constituency—based on their conclusions from your work. This whole spectrum of ways of acting is legitimate and can be effective in addressing your problematic situation.

The contribution of the scenario project is not that it has "gotten" actors to act—this is what they have been doing and continue to do. Instead, its contribution is to help actors to act with broader and deeper and more aligned understandings, relationships, and intentions—with greater wisdom. The Dalai Lama articulated this premise when he argued that his insight into the complexities of the relationship between China and Tibet justified his controversial nonaggressive stance toward China: "Holistic understanding brings realistic action."[7]

Transformative scenario planning inspires actions by concentric circles of change agents. The first circle is made up of the members of your scenario team itself: you are the ones who make the biggest impact on the process and are the most affected by it. This is why your selection of the members of the team was such a crucial step in the process.

The next circle includes people with whom your team members engage. You can do this in many ways: you can engage one-on-one in private conversations or briefings with key individuals, including ones from your own organization or sector. You can engage in meetings or workshops with the teams of leaders of key organizations, including your own. You can have in-person or virtual dialogues or town hall meetings with large gatherings of fellow citizens. And you can connect with larger populations through print, broadcast, and social media, and through working with cultural agents.

You should consider all these engagements not simply as ways to *distribute* the scenario team's inert products but rather as means to *disseminate*—to plant seeds that contain—the team's generative understandings, relationships, and intentions. You want other people to be inspired to pick these seeds up, to work with them, and to act on them. Transformative scenario planning contributes to transforming systems only if the seeds it produces propagate and spread.

Whatever combination of joint and separate actions you choose to take, you need to maintain in some form the container and infrastructure that the project has created. This will help you to support the continued actions, including spinoff activities, by the team and others who have become involved in the work. It will also help you to enable ongoing inspiration, learning, and mutual assistance among these people.

You have now produced the intended outputs of your project. You have grown systemic understandings, cross-system relationships, and system-aware intentions. Through these results, you have enabled actors who together have the capacity to transform the system to take wiser action to do so. Most fundamentally, you have opened up a way for the actors to get unstuck and move forward, collaboratively and creatively, with energy and momentum, to deal with their situation.

8

New Stories Can Generate
New Realities

*T*HERE IS NO EASY OR STRAIGHTFORWARD or
guaranteed way to transform complex social
systems. My own experience of 20 years of working with transformative scenario planning processes has been of producing both failure and success—or, more accurately, of not really
knowing whether the processes have produced failure or success.
Transformative scenario planning contributes to transforming
systems through contributing to transforming actors and their
actions. I can now see that this process is not as direct or immediate as I thought it was right after Mont Fleur. Poet Gil Scott-
Heron said: "The first revolution is when you change your mind
about how you look at things. The revolution—that change that
takes place—will not be televised."[1] Transformative scenario
planning generates tangible and visible change in the world via
subtle, invisible, and nonlinear changes within and among us.

My most instructive experience of these ambiguities in making
out the impacts of this work has been in Colombia. The Destino
Colombia scenario project was conceived in 1995 but was almost
stillborn; in 1996 it suddenly came to life; in 1997 the scenario
team held three energetic workshops; in 1998 and 1999 they disseminated their results to the whole country; in 2004 the project
was pronounced dormant or dead; in 2007 I heard stories about

the project's continued influence; and in 2012 the president of Colombia announced that it had always been alive and was now the leitmotif of the policies of his new government.[2] What I have learned from this experience and others is that you must try to do this work as best you can, but that its failure or success—like most things about the future—cannot be controlled or predicted or even known. The Hindu text *The Bhagavad Gita* puts it succinctly: "The work is yours, but not the fruits thereof."[3]

Colombia has a long history of violent conflict. It has a home-grown academic discipline called violentology. In the first half of the 1900s, it had two bloody civil wars, the second one simply called "The Violence." Beginning in the 1960s, it suffered continuing clashes among the military, drug traffickers, criminal gangs, left-wing guerrilla forces, and right-wing paramilitary vigilantes, which were characterized by kidnappings, executions, massacres, and no-go areas. At the same time, the country maintained democratic governments, a dynamic business sector, and an active civil society. It has faced enormous challenges and also has demonstrated enormous capacities to address these challenges.

In 1995, businessman Manuel José Carvajal read about Mont Fleur and thought that a transformative scenario planning project might help Colombians to discover new ways out of their conflict. He discussed this idea with people he knew and to whom he was introduced, but he was not getting enough support to get the project off the ground. He was about to give up on the effort when he talked with Juan Manuel Santos, a journalist turned politician who had independently been pursuing the same idea. Within a few weeks, the two of them organized a large meeting of national actors to see what interest there might be in such a process.

The meeting included top leaders from politics, business, the military, the church, and academia, plus guerrillas participating by telephone from a secret location. The participants were both excited and nervous to find themselves in such an unusually heterogeneous group. One Communist Party city councilor, spotting a paramilitary warlord across the room, asked Santos: "Do you really expect me to sit down with this man, who has tried to have me killed five times?" Santos replied: "It is precisely so that he does not do so a sixth time that I am inviting you to take your seat."[4]

I was also excited to be at the meeting and bewildered by the extraordinary questions such a proposed exercise raised. After I had given a presentation about the Mont Fleur experience, a question from one of the guerrillas was relayed to me by phone: "Do we have to agree to a ceasefire to participate in the scenario workshops?" I gave an answer that I hoped was correct: "A scenario process is not a negotiation. There are no preconditions to participating except a willingness to talk and to listen."

Santos understood that he was too partisan a figure to be able to convene such a transpartisan process, and at the end of the meeting he stepped back, and a broader and more neutral organizing committee stepped forward. The committee's objective was to put together a scenario team that would be representative of the whole conflicted society and in particular would enable the combatants to talk with one another directly. To do this, the committee had to decide whom they considered to be legitimate players with plausible commitments to the future of the country, and who was too criminal or corrupt. They ended up including in the team guerrillas and paramilitaries, as well as academics, activists, businesspeople, journalists, military officers, peasants, politicians, trade unionists, and young people. They excluded drug traffickers and people from the administration of then president Ernesto Samper, whose election campaign was thought to have been partly financed by traffickers. (Later, Carvajal said that he thought this attempt to be "aseptic" had been counterproductive because it resulted in the team's work being ignored by the government until after the end of Samper's term.)

The scenario team met three times over four months, in total for ten days, at a lovely old farm called Recinto Quirama, in the rolling green hills outside of Medellin. We had the whole spread-out property to ourselves: a high-ceilinged barn for a meeting room; an open-air, cobbled-floor dining room and bar; a swimming pool; and simple sleeping rooms surrounded by flower gardens. I arrived a day before the start of the first workshop and was amazed to find such tranquillity in the midst of such conflict. Then I went for a swim in the pool and emerged to find it surrounded by soldiers with machine guns, protecting the meeting from attack.

The most remarkable feature of the project was the participation of both of the illegal, armed, left-wing guerrilla groups: the FARC (Revolutionary Armed Forces of Colombia) and the ELN (National Liberation Army). Although the government had offered them safe passage to the workshops, the guerrillas thought that this would be too risky, and so we arranged, extraordinarily, for them to participate in the team's meetings by telephone. Three men called in from the political prisoners' wing of a maximum-security prison and one from exile in Costa Rica. This arrangement produced some surreal moments, such as when one of the guerrillas called in from a prison pay phone, saying that he had enough coins for only a few minutes but wanted to offer his input on the draft scenarios.

Many of the team members were terrified because they were talking with the guerrillas for the first time. We communicated using two speakerphones in the meeting room. When people walked by the speakerphones, they gave the phones a wide berth, afraid to get too close. Some of the participants were frightened of retribution for what they might say to the guerrillas. When I mentioned this fear, one of the guerrillas observed that our microcosm was reflecting the macrocosm: "Mr. Kahane, why are you surprised that people in the room are frightened? The whole country is frightened." Then the guerrillas promised they would not kill anyone for anything said in the meetings.

The team came up with a set of ground rules for their work together. They agreed to speak frankly; to express their differences without irony; to assume the good faith of others; to be tolerant, disciplined, and punctual; to be concrete and concise; and to keep confidences. They were proud of these ground rules, which in the midst of so much lawlessness and violence helped them to construct a strong and safe container. Within this container, the team members were gradually able to open up and deepen their relationships. After a while, during breaks in the meetings, participants huddled around the speakerphones, continuing to talk with the guerrillas. One team member later said:

> Never have such diverse people in Colombia done so much together. It is very difficult to bring into the same process the extremes that are tearing apart the country and who beforehand had made it clear that they would not have any dealings with one another. For each of the extremes, the other does not exist or should cease to exist. We succeeded in this process of dialogue, of respecting the rules of the game, and of improving the way we treat one another, our manner of conversing, and the quality of our long-term thinking.[5]

Another said:

> War produces something that is quite complicated to understand: the absence of tolerance. War as such is a drastic solution to all problems. It is the maximum solution, and in this situation it is hard to be tolerant of the ideas of others. This scenario methodology compels you to accept that the solution may be different from what you have thought.[6]

Jaime Caicedo was the secretary general of the far-left Communist Party of Colombia, and Iván Duque was a commander of the far-right paramilitary United Self-Defense Forces of Colombia (AUC). One evening, Caicedo and Duque stayed up late talking and drinking and playing the guitar with Juan Salcedo, a retired army general. The next morning, Caicedo wasn't there in the meeting room when we were due to start, and I asked the group where he was. There were lots of jokes about what might have happened to him. One person said: "The general made him sing." Then Duque said, menacingly, "I saw him last." I was terrified that Caicedo had been murdered and was relieved when a few minutes later he walked into the room.

(Many years later, I heard a revealing coda to this story. Duque had gone into the jungle to meet his boss, Carlos Castaño, the notorious head of AUC. Castaño excitedly told Duque that AUC fighters had discovered the location of their arch-enemy Caicedo and were on their way to assassinate him. Duque pleaded for Caicedo's life, telling Castaño the story of that evening together at the scenario workshop and saying: "You can't kill him: we were on the Destino Colombia team together." After much arguing, Castaño called off the assassination. This story exemplifies the transformative potential of these processes: to be willing to defy Castaño on this matter of life and death, Duque must have transformed his sense of his relationship with Caicedo and of what he himself needed to stand for and do.)

As the work progressed, the team members became less afraid and more willing to speak frankly. At one point, a landowner said that he had had a lot of firsthand experience of the conflict with the guerrillas, that he did not trust them at all, and that he believed the country's best hope for peace would be to intensify the military campaign against them. It took courage for him to say this because he was directly challenging not only the guerrillas but also the rest of the team and their hopeful belief that a negotiated solution was possible. He was willing to be open and confrontational. But by now, the team's relationships and the project's container were strong enough to hear such a statement without rupturing. Furthermore, when he said exactly what he was thinking and feeling, the fog of conceptual and emotional confusion that had filled the room lifted, and we could all see an important dynamic in the team and in the country.

By the end of their third workshop, the team had agreed on four scenarios. The first, "When the Sun Rises We'll See," was a warning of the chaos that would result if Colombians just let things be and failed to address their tough challenges. The second, "A Bird in the Hand Is Worth Two in the Bush," was a story of a negotiated compromise between the government and the guerrillas. The third, "Forward March!," was a story of the government, supported by a population frustrated with the continuing violence and operating from the principle that "a hard problem requires a hard solution," implementing a policy of crushing the guerrillas militarily and pacifying the country (this was the possible future revealed by the landowner's statement). The fourth, "In Unity Lies Strength," was a story of a bottom-up transformation of the country's mentality toward greater mutual respect and cooperation.

The team disseminated their scenarios on a massive scale. They published a summary of their work as an insert in all the country's major newspapers, created a video that was shown on national television, and held large public meetings in all the regional capitals. The stories were taken up in the strategic conversation of many governmental, business, and community organizations, but I never heard of any signs of these seeds germinating and taking root. My inference was that although transformation had occurred in some of the team members and in some of the relationships among them, this transformation had not had a systemic impact. In a 2006 report, political scientist Angelika Rettberg reached a similar conclusion: "The greatest impact was on those who participated, changing their perceptions, attitudes, and stereotypes, and generating a mutually enriching human approach to the construction of peace. But the impact seems to be diminished when we look at the participants in their professional lives and at broader public policy decisions and social processes."[7] And a 2004 report by Alfredo de León and Elena Díez Pinto for the United Nations Development Programme labeled Destino Colombia "a treasure still to be revealed."[8]

When the Sun Rises
We'll See

A Bird in the Hand Is
Worth Two in the Bush

Forward March!

In Unity Lies Strength

The Destino Colombia Scenarios, 1997

I was therefore taken aback when in 2007 I talked with Antanas Mockus, a leading intellectual, two-term mayor of Bogotá, and presidential candidate. His view was that Colombia had been systematically working through the four scenarios. In 1998, Ernesto Samper's successor, President Andrés Pastrana, had tried and failed to achieve a negotiated settlement like the one described in "A Bird in the Hand Is Worth Two in the Bush." In 2002, this failure produced the wave of popular frustration that brought President Álvaro Uribe to power, and he was now implementing a military pacification of the country like the one described in "Forward March!" Mockus's hypothesis was that some businesspeople and landowners, having concluded that "Forward March!" was the best option for themselves and for the country, had proposed it as a blueprint to the Uribe government. He told me: "We must not fix our attention only on the conviviality of such dialogue processes. We must not forget the harsher external world, where scenarios can be chosen to guide action." Now he wanted to understand how the fourth scenario, "In Unity Lies Strength," could be implemented.[9]

In 2012, I returned to Colombia to launch the Spanish edition of my book *Power and Love*. The country was doing well: economic investment and output were up; poverty and violence were down. A series of high-level multistakeholder dialogues, inspired in part by "In Unity Lies Strength," had produced an "Agenda for Colombia" that included important policy reforms on land rights, fair economic growth, and compensation for the victims of armed conflict. *Time* magazine had just published a cover story titled "The Colombian Comeback." Juan Manuel Santos, who 16 years before had put together the organizing meeting for Destino Colombia and who 2 years before had beaten Mockus to be elected president of the country, gave a speech at the book launch. He said:

> When we held the organizing meeting for Destino Colombia in 1996, the country was talking of

nothing except the drug case against President Samper, and there were no new proposals for progress on other important issues such as the armed conflict and political polarization of the country. . . . Never before this meeting had such a broad group been convened, with such diverse and important sectors of Colombian society—many of them absolute opponents or enemies, who had killed and were continuing to kill each other—to find an approach to end the conflict. . . .

It is truly breathtaking to read the Destino Colombia scenarios now, because they seem more prophetic than academic. . . . The first scenario, "When the Sun Rises We'll See," invited us to think about what would happen if, instead of making a timely intervention, Colombians left the country's problems to resolve themselves, which led to a loss of state authority, an upsurge of violence, territorial fragmentation, and a dramatic increase in poverty and social inequality. The second scenario, "A Bird in the Hand Is Worth Two in the Bush," alluded to concessions being offered to the armed groups to start to rebuild democracy and to stop—at all costs—the increasing cycle of death and violence. Today, as we mark ten years since the end of the major negotiations with the guerrillas, we know that this scenario was attempted but failed, and not because of an unwillingness of the government or of the Colombian people, but because of the obstinacy of the guerrillas' violence and terrorist acts. This resulted in some of the characteristics of the third scenario, "Forward March!," in which the political leadership acts on the popular demand to restore security and assumes a mandate that is characterized by firmness against the violent. . . . Faced with such clear evidence, who can deny the prophetic gifts of those who met at Recinto Quirama!

In Colombia, we have now embarked on an irrevers-
ible evolutionary process that we hope will culminate
in the peaceful transition and the final reconsolida-
tion of the fourth scenario, "In Unity Lies Strength."
That scenario is the way forward that we want to realize today with the National Unity proposal that my
government has launched. . . . It is good to know that
the best scenario that we imagined 16 years ago is now
beginning to be realized.[10]

With this speech, Santos was placing Destino Colombia—
both the methodology it had used for working across differences
and the stories it had told about Colombia's choices—at the center of his narrative about what was unfolding in Colombia. He
was also placing it at the center of his narrative about his own
lifetime political project, which he characterized—with respect
to the way he worked with other actors: other politicians, civil
society, international allies, the guerrillas—as combining "the
positive drive of power, which invites us to growth and self-real-
ization, with that of love, which invites us to unite that which is
separated." He understood that "this combination is essential for
countries who have suffered deep wounds, like ours, to be able to
overcome their conflict and to build together a better future." He
differentiated his approach from those of his predecessors Pastrana (more love than power) and Uribe (more power than love).
The stories that the Destino Colombia team had told about their
country had become interwoven with the stories of its leaders.

Betty Sue Flowers is a poet and a student of myth who started
writing scenario stories with me at Shell in 1991. I told her about
Santos's remarkable speech, and she reminded me of how skeptical I had been back then of our colleague Joseph Jaworski's
effort to use scenarios not only to study the future but to shift
it. (Shell had rejected this effort at the time but embraced it in
2008 when the company advocated for "Blueprints," a scenario
of global actors working together to address the challenges of

global warming.[11]) "Scenarios can mutate into empowering myths," Betty Sue told me. "Myths give us courage. If it is already true in the story, then, paradoxically, we can make it happen." As we tell and live new stories, we change what can happen in the world around us.

On the same day in 2012 that Santos made this speech, I met with Francisco Galán, one of the ELN guerrillas who had participated in all of the Destino Colombia meetings by telephone from prison. In 2008, he had been released from prison, and he was now working on both high-level and grassroots peace efforts. He struck me as a man who, from much hard-won experience, had achieved a measure of wisdom and peacefulness. "I have learned," he said, "that it is more difficult to make peace than to make war." He went on: "If we keep repeating the same stories about our country, then we will keep doing the same things, which do not work. But we are addicted to this repetition! We need to get fed up with these same stories. We need new stories."

9

The Inner Game of Social Transformation

*W*E OFTEN TELL OURSELVES that we can succeed in transforming the future through forceful action. Increasingly often, however, we cannot. As the world becomes more complex, with more interdependency and more unpredictability and more actors with power and voice, it becomes more difficult to effect transformation unilaterally. We need new stories.

The story of transformative scenario planning is one of collaboration instead of unilateralism. Most of the projects described in this book were motivated by a need for collaboration. Many of these projects produced hopeful scenarios of increasing collaboration, including "In Unity Lies Strength" in Colombia, "Flight of the Fireflies" in Guatemala, "Portage" in Canada, "Final Dawning" in Sudan, and "Flight of the Flamingos" and "Walk Together" in South Africa. And all the projects employed a process characterized by collaboration that enabled (rather than forced) actors to choose to transform themselves. The example of the Destino Colombia process enabling Iván Duque's transformation of himself and his situation is only the most dramatic of many.

Transformative scenario planning is one of a family of stories about how to transform social systems collaboratively. These include all kinds of ways to live and work together without violence or aggression, in families, teams, organizations, communities, and countries. Transformative scenario planning is a particularly effective way for a team of actors to generate collaborative forward movement on a complex, stuck, problematic situation. What does it take, working in this way, to succeed in transforming the future?

Sports psychologist Tim Gallwey says: "In every human endeavor there are two arenas of engagement: the outer and the inner. The outer game is played on an external arena to overcome external obstacles to reach an external goal. The inner game takes place within the mind of the player."[1]

The *outer game* of transformative scenario planning is for the team to generate forward movement by taking the five steps outlined in the previous chapters: convening, observing, constructing, discovering, and acting. Through these steps, they combine three inputs—a whole-system team, a strong container, and a rigorous process—to produce the four outputs—transformed understandings, relationships, intentions, and actions. What it takes to succeed in this outer game is the ability to manage this ambitious and complicated set of political, intellectual, and organizational activities.

The *inner game* of transformative scenario planning, on the other hand, is for the team to generate this forward movement without pushing. It is to effect systemic transformation purposefully, passionately, and with commitment, while at the same time flexibly, dispassionately, and without attachment. Artist Jeff Barnum says that the essence of such a creative stance is "intent without content: remaining structured, dynamic, and purposeful in a space of not knowing."[2]

What it takes to succeed in the inner game of transformative scenario planning is the ability to work with the tension and ambiguity of being both directed and open. Winston Churchill said that engaging with Russia required dealing with "a riddle wrapped in a mystery inside an enigma."[3] Succeeding in the inner game of transformative scenario planning requires dealing with a mystery wrapped in a dilemma inside a paradox.

A *paradox* is a proposition that appears to be self-contradictory. The paradox of transformative scenario planning is that we move forward by stepping back. We get unstuck not by pushing but instead by pausing. We deal with situations that seem to demand urgent action by instead employing deliberate talk. The Sudanese leader Pagan Amum wanted a scenario workshop because it would create such a pause in the rush to war. We transform the future by approaching it indirectly via a creative and hence open and ambiguous detour. Writer André Gide said: "One doesn't discover new lands without consenting to lose sight of the shore for a very long time."[4]

The fundamental capacity required to deal with this paradox is *suspending*. Suspending means taking our thoughts about our situation and hanging them in front of us, as if from a string. This enables us and others to notice and investigate our thoughts, so that we can, if necessary, alter them. Suspending is the doorway into the creative "U" process.[5] Failing to suspend locks us into reenacting old realities rather than enacting new ones. It was such a reenactment of old conversations and roles that the organizer of the Canadian project feared and that later occurred.

Suspending assumes and acknowledges that there is not only one way to look at what is happening or should happen. Amid the extreme, stuck polarization among the factions in Zimbabwe, each with its own one way, the scenario team recognized that suspending would allow them to see beyond their durawalls, and so they seized on this practice as their primary tool for getting unstuck. When we suspend, we allow ourselves to change, and as we change, we open up new avenues for others to do the same.

The simple act of suspending is the key to collaborative social transformation because it is the necessary first step to working creatively with diverse others. It is the key to transformative scenario planning in particular because in this process we work with multiple stories about what could happen, rather than any single story about what will happen (a forecast) or what should happen (a proposal). "Scenarios," Betty Sue Flowers says, "are like different lenses through which we can see the world."[6] Multiple stories generate possibilities for new futures. Ever since the brainstorming of 30 stories during the first Mont Fleur workshop, I have repeatedly been struck by how dramatically suspending and storytelling unlock the door to collaboration, creativity, and forward movement.

Suspending is simple, but it is not easy. It requires us to place in doubt the comforting belief that we know what is going on and are in control. It therefore opens up the frightening possibility that we are lost and in danger. This is what Howard Gabriels felt at Mont Fleur when he thought through scenarios that he had never before been willing to consider. Those of us who are accustomed to believing that we know and are in control experience this possibility of not knowing as disorienting and disturbing—especially when we are in high-pressure, high-stakes situations. To succeed in the inner game, we need to be willing to sit with this uncertainty and ambiguity.

Inside this paradox is a *dilemma*. A dilemma is a situation where we face two apparently opposed imperatives and we must work with both.[7] The dilemma of transformative scenario planning is that within the paradox of pausing to advance, we must work with two drives that are in permanent tension: love and power. Love is the drive to open up and connect to other ideas and actors and possibilities. We need to exercise love to create the potential to transform our thinking and acting and so to transform the system. Power, on the other hand, is the drive to realize one's potential and to grow. We need to exercise power to actualize the potential we create.[8]

We often experience love and power to be in conflict. Most people incorrectly infer that they must choose one or the other. But choosing either love or power is always a mistake and always leaves us stuck.

Choosing only opening and connecting, and ignoring or denying realizing and growing, produces a warm and friendly feeling among the actors but smothers difference and potential. This choice produces a timid and ungrounded consensus that is useful neither to the actors nor to the system. Martin Luther King Jr. said of such results: "Love without power is sentimental and anemic." On the other hand, choosing only realizing and growing, and ignoring or denying opening and connecting, leaves each actor rigidly unchanged within his or her own perspective and plan. This choice therefore prevents us from transforming ourselves and thereby our system. King said of such results: "Power without love is reckless and abusive."[9] We can transform social systems collaboratively only if we choose both love and power.

We work with power and love in transformative scenario planning by working with wholes and parts. On the one hand, we treat each social entity we are working with (for example, each person) as a complete whole in itself, with its own integral and legitimate perspective and interests and evolution, thereby taking account of the entity's power drive. On the other hand, we treat each entity as part of the perspective and interests and evolution of larger wholes (for example, communities), thereby taking account of the entity's love drive.

This attention to multiple wholes produces a permanent creative tension. In working with the Dinokeng team, I noticed that we found our way forward by alternating between emphasizing the smaller whole (the perspective of each person) until the team became fragmented, and emphasizing the larger whole (the consensus of the team) until we fell into groupthink.[10] In scenario work, we must not privilege any smaller whole (such as one powerful person) over any larger one (such as the team). Nor must we privilege any larger whole over any smaller one, such as by demanding that someone "put aside their agenda" to benefit "the good of the team." We must never choose either whole; we must always choose both, alternately. What this requires of us as leaders or facilitators is the capacity to embrace and exercise both our power and our love.

Wrapped in this dilemma, finally, is a *mystery*. A mystery is something that cannot be known. The mystery at the heart of transformative scenario planning is that we cannot know the future. We can investigate it and influence it, but we cannot calculate it or control it. We can and must plan and prepare and practice, but we cannot know what the outcome of our efforts will be.

These ambiguities and challenges, however, need not and must not prevent us from acting. If we are not content to accept or adapt to what is happening, then we have no choice: we must step in. If we can do this together, with commitment and openness to what is needed of us, then we can succeed in creating better futures.

Resources: Transformative
Scenario Planning Processes

*T*HOSE UNDERTAKING transformative scenario planning projects have available to them many options for processes to use in each of the five steps. This page lists the processes referred to in chapters 3 through 7. Other resources are available at www.reospartners.com/scenarios.

FIRST STEP: CONVENE A TEAM FROM ACROSS THE SYSTEM

- Seek out potential allies
- Identify and enroll a convening team and then a scenario team
- Conduct dialogue interviews of scenario team members and other actors
- Make a project plan and mobilize necessary resources
- Build the project container

SECOND STEP: OBSERVE WHAT IS HAPPENING

- Share and reflect in the scenario team
- Go on learning journeys
- Commission research papers
- Interact with resource people

- Search for structural driving forces
- List certainties and uncertainties

Third step: Construct stories about what could happen

- Choose key certainties and uncertainties
- Construct scenarios deductively
- Construct scenarios inductively
- Write logical narratives of hypothetical future events
- Find metaphors, images, and names for each scenario
- Create pictures that compare and contrast the scenarios
- Document the scenarios in different media

Fourth step: Discover what can and must be done

- Take an adaptive stance
- Take a transformative stance
- Consider your strengths and weaknesses in, and the opportunities and threats of, each scenario
- Develop options for joint and separate actions
- Draw conclusions about what you will do

Fifth step: Act to transform the system

- Hold individual, organizational, and public meetings
- Disseminate the scenario using print, broadcast, and social media
- Launch spinoff initiatives
- Cultivate and coordinate an ongoing network of inspired and aligned actors

Notes

PREFACE

1. The adaptive scenario planning methodology is explained in Jeremy B. Bentham et al., *Scenarios: An Explorer's Guide* (The Hague: Shell International, 2008); Thomas Chermack, *Scenario Planning in Organizations: How to Create, Use, and Assess Scenarios* (San Francisco: Berrett-Koehler Publishers, 2011); Rafael Ramírez, John W. Selsky, and Kees van der Heijden, eds., *Business Planning for Turbulent Times: New Methods for Applying Scenarios* (London: Routledge, 2010); Diana Scearce and Katherine Fulton, *What If?: The Art of Scenario Thinking for Nonprofits* (San Francisco: Global Business Network, 2004); Peter Schwartz, *The Art of the Long View: Planning for the Future in an Uncertain World* (New York: Currency, 1996); Chantell Ilbury and Clem Sunter, *Mind of a Fox: Scenario Planning in Action* (Cape Town, South Africa: Human & Rousseau, 2001); Kees van der Heijden, *Scenarios: The Art of Strategic Conversation* (Chichester, West Sussex, England: John Wiley & Sons, 1996); and Kees van der Heijden et al., *The Sixth Sense: Accelerating Organizational Learning with Scenarios* (Chichester, West Sussex, England: John Wiley & Sons, 2002). The transformative scenario planning methodology is referred to in Barbara Heinzen, *Feeling for Stones: Learning and Invention When Facing the Unknown* (London: Barbara Heinzen, 2006); Barbara Heinzen, *How Do Societies Learn?* (London: Barbara Heinzen, 2009); Barbara Heinzen, ed., *Surviving Uncertainty*, Society for International Development, *Development* 47, no. 4 (2004); Katrin Käufer, "Learning from the Civic Scenario Project: A Tool for Facilitating Social Change?" in Katrin Käufer et al., *Learning Histories: Democratic Dialogue Regional Project*, Working Paper 3 (New York: United Nations Development Programme Regional Bureau for Latin America and the Caribbean, 2004); James A. Ogilvy, *Creating Better Futures: Scenario Planning as a Tool for a Better Tomorrow* (New

York: Oxford University Press, 2002); and Angela Wilkinson and Esther Eidenow, "Evolving Practices in Environmental Scenarios: A New Scenario Typology," *Environmental Research Letters 3* (2008).

CHAPTER 1: AN INVENTION BORN OF NECESSITY

1. See van der Heijden, *Scenarios*; Art Kleiner, *The Age of Heretics: Heroes, Outlaws, and the Forerunners of Corporate Change* (New York: Doubleday, 1996) and "The Man Who Saw the Future," *strategy+business* 30 (2003); Pierre Wack, "Scenarios: Shooting the Rapids," *Harvard Business Review* 63, no. 6 (1985), and "Scenarios: Uncharted Waters Ahead," *Harvard Business Review* 63, no. 5 (1985); and Angela Wilkinson and Roland Kupers, *Re-perceiving Scenarios: The Evolution of the Gentle Art in Shell 1965–2010*, ed. Betty Sue Flowers (forthcoming in 2012).

2. Clem Sunter, *The World and South Africa in the 1990s* (Cape Town, South Africa: Tafelberg, 1987).

3. See Pieter le Roux, Vincent Maphai, et al., "The Mont Fleur Scenarios," *Deeper News* 7, no. 1 (1992); Nick Segal, *Breaking the Mould: The Role of Scenarios in Shaping South Africa's Future* (Stellenbosch, South Africa: Sun Press, 2007); and Glennifer Gillespie, "The Footprints of Mont Fleur: The Mont Fleur Scenario Project, South Africa, 1991–1992," in Käufer et al., *Learning Histories*.

4. Unpublished project document, 2000.

5. Unpublished project document, 2000.

6. Gillespie, "The Footprints of Mont Fleur," 36.

7. Le Roux et al., "The Mont Fleur Scenarios."

8. Segal, *Breaking the Mould*, 49.

9. Personal communication with Pieter le Roux, 2012.

10. Gillespie, "The Footprints of Mont Fleur," 41.

11. Personal communication with Pieter le Roux, 2012.

12. Allister Sparks, *Beyond the Miracle: Inside the New South Africa* (Johannesburg, South Africa: Jonathan Bell Publishers, 2003), 170.

13. Unpublished project document, 2000.

14. Clem Sunter, "The Icarus Scenario," news24.com, January 20, 2010.

15. Personal communication with Rob Davies, 1992.

Chapter 2: A New Way to Work with the Future

1. I am referring here to the consequences of social, dynamic, and generative complexity respectively. See Adam Kahane, *Power and Love: A Theory and Practice of Social Change* (San Francisco: Berrett-Koehler Publishers, 2009), 5; and Peter Senge and Otto Scharmer, "Community Action Research: Learning as a Community of Practitioners, Consultants and Researchers," in Peter Reason and Hilary Bradbury, eds., *Handbook of Action Research: Participative Inquiry and Practice* (Thousand Oaks, CA: Sage Publications, 2001), 23.

2. I learned this crucial distinction between problems and problematic situations from Kees van der Heijden.

3. Brian Arthur says that new technologies arise from new and unexpected combinations of existing ones. See W. Brian Arthur, *The Nature of Technology: What It Is and How It Evolves* (New York: Free Press, 2009).

4. This container principle is explained in Crane Wood Stookey, *Keep Your People in the Boat: Workforce Engagement Lessons from the Sea* (Halifax: Nova Scotia: ALIA Press, 2012).

5. The U-Process is outlined in Peter Senge et al., *Presence: Human Purpose and the Field of the Future* (New York: Broadway Business, 2008), and Otto Scharmer, *Theory U: Leading from the Future as It Emerges* (San Francisco: Berrett-Koehler Publishers, 2009). I have also learned about the U-Process from Jeff Barnum.

6. Personal communication with Bill O'Brien, 2000. Also see William O'Brien, *Character at Work: Building Prosperity Through the Practice of Virtue* (Boston: Paulist Press, 2008).

Chapter 3: First Step: Convene a Team from Across the Whole System

1. See Choice Ndoro et al., *The Great Zimbabwe Scenarios: A Map of Four Possible Futures* (Harare, Zimbabwe: The Great Zimbabwe Scenarios Project, 2012).

2. Unpublished project document, 2011.

Chapter 4: Second Step: Observe What Is Happening

1. See Commission for Historical Clarification, *Guatemala: Memory of Silence—Report of the Commission for Historical Clarification* (Washington, DC: American Association for the Advancement of Science, 1999).

2. See Elena Díez Pinto et al., *Los Escenarios del Futuro* [Scenarios of the future] (Guatemala City, Guatemala: Visión Guatemala, 1999), and Elena Díez Pinto, "Building Bridges of Trust: Visión Guatemala, 1998–2000," in Käufer et al., *Learning Histories.* See also Kahane, *Power and Love*, 32–35, 42–46, and 113–27.

3. Elena Díez Pinto, "Building Bridges of Trust," 45.

4. Ibid., 47.

5. Daniel Coates et al., "An Invitation to Participate in a Strategic Dialogue about Canada's Future" (Almonte, Ontario, Canada: The Scenarios for the Future Project, 1998).

6. See Ofer Zalzberg, *EU Partnership for Peace—Israeli Track* (London: Oxford Research Group, 2009), and Kahane, *Power and Love*, 75–87.

7. Zalzberg, *EU Partnership for Peace*, 1.

8. Personal communication with Tova Averbuch, 2008.

9. William Gibson, "The Science in Science Fiction," *Talk of the Nation*, National Public Radio, November 30, 1999.

10. Hardin Tibbs, "Pierre Wack: A Remarkable Source of Insight," *Netview* 9 (1998), 8.

11. I learned this formulation from Louis van der Merwe.

12. Kleiner, "The Man Who Saw the Future," 2.

13 One excellent tool is Lego Serious Play, which I learned how to use from Per Kristiansen.

14. See Peter Senge, *The Fifth Discipline: The Art & Practice of the Learning Organization* (New York: Broadway Business, 2006).

CHAPTER 5: THIRD STEP: CONSTRUCT STORIES ABOUT WHAT COULD HAPPEN

1. Unpublished project document, 2011.

2. Paula Cristina Roque and Paul-Simon Handy, *Sudan Scenarios to Strategies Workshop* (Pretoria, South Africa: Institute for Security Studies, 2010).

3. Ibid., 3

4. These and other methods for constructing scenarios are elaborated in van der Heijden, *Scenarios*; Schwartz, *The Art of the Long View*; and Lawrence Wilkinson, "How to Build Scenarios," *Wired* (September 1995).

5. Whereas in adaptive scenario planning you work with the uncertainties that have impact and are unpredictable, in transformative scenario planning you work with the ones that have impact, are unpredictable, and are also influenceable. I am indebted to Antonio Aranibar for this important insight.

6. See Wilkinson and Kupers, *Re-perceiving Scenarios*.

CHAPTER 6: FOURTH STEP: DISCOVER WHAT CAN AND MUST BE DONE

1. Mamphela Ramphele et al., *The Dinokeng Scenarios: Three Futures for South Africa* (Johannesburg, South Africa: Dinokeng Scenarios, 2009).

2. Coates et al., *An Invitation to Participate in a Strategic Dialogue*.

3. This point was made to me by Bill Tolbert.

CHAPTER 7: FIFTH STEP: ACT TO TRANSFORM THE SYSTEM

1. Trevor Manuel, speech to the AGRISA Conference on New Challenges in Agriculture, Stellenbosch, South Africa, February 21, 2012.

2. Unpublished project document, 2010.

3. Mamphela Ramphele, speech at the launch of the North Star Scenarios, East London, South Africa, April 26, 2012.

4. Personal communication with Lars Franklin, 2000.

5. Díez, "Building Bridges of Trust," 99–100.

6. Ibid., 102.

7. Evan Osnos, "The Next Incarnation," *New Yorker*, October 4, 2010, 71.

CHAPTER 8: NEW STORIES CAN GENERATE NEW REALITIES

1. Gil Scott-Heron, in *Gil Scott-Heron: Black Wax*, film by Robert Mugge, 1982.

2. See Manuel José Carvajal et al., "Destino Colombia: A Scenario-Planning Process for the New Millennium," *Deeper News* 9, no. 1 (1998); Angelika Rettberg, *Destino Colombia: Crónica y evaluación de un ejercicio de participación de líderes de la sociedad civil en el diseño de escenarios futuros* [Destination Colombia: Chronicle and evaluation of an exercise of civil society leaders in the design of future scenar-

ios] (Bogotá, Colombia: Ediciones Uniandes, 2006); Alfredo de León and Elena Díez Pinto, "A Treasure to Be Revealed: Destino Colombia, 1997–2000," in Käufer et al., *Learning Histories*; and Juan Manuel Santos, "Palabras del Presidente Juan Manuel Santos en la presentación del libro *Poder y Amor* de Adam Kahane" [Remarks of President Juan Manuel Santos at the presentation of the book *Power and Love*, by Adam Kahane], Bogotá, Colombia, February 21, 2012.

3. Eknath Easwaren, trans., *The Bhagavad Gita* (Tomales, CA: Nilgiri Press, 1998), chapter 2, verse 47.

4. Juan Manuel Santos, "Presentacíon" [Presentation], in Adam Kahane, *Poder y Amor: Teoría y Práctica para el Cambio Social* [Power and Love: A Theory and Practice of Social Change] (La Paz, Bolivia: Plural, 2011), 14.

5. De León and Díez, "A Treasure to Be Revealed," 58.

6. Ibid., 61.

7. Rettberg, *Destino Colombia*, 70.

8. De León and Díez, "A Treasure to Be Revealed," 51.

9. Personal communication with Antanas Mockus, 2007.

10. Santos, "Palabras del Presidente Juan Manuel Santos."

11. Jeroen van der Veer, "Exploring the Reasons for Strategic Change," speech at the European Universities Association conference at Erasmus University, Rotterdam, the Netherlands, November 20, 2008.

CHAPTER 9: THE INNER GAME OF SOCIAL TRANSFORMATION

1. The Inner Game (www.theinnergame.com). My thanks to Zaid Hassan for pointing out the ways in which collaborative social transformation processes are team sports.

2. Personal communication with Jeff Barnum, 2012.

3. Winston Churchill, "The Russian Enigma," BBC broadcast, October 1, 1939.

4. André Gide, *The Counterfeiters: A Novel* (New York: Vintage, 1973), 353.

5. Otto Scharmer explains this with reference to the thinking of Francisco Varela in *Theory U*, 36.

6. Personal communication with Betty Sue Flowers, 1991.

7. See Charles Hampden-Turner, *Charting the Corporate Mind* (New York: Blackwell Publishing, 1993), and Barry Johnson, *Polarity Management: Identifying and Managing Unsolvable Problems* (Amherst, MA: HRD Press, 1996).

8. See Kahane, *Power and Love.*

9. King made these statements in Martin Luther King Jr., "Where Do We Go from Here?" in *A Call to Conscience: The Landmark Speeches of Dr. Martin Luther King, Jr.*, ed. Clayborne Carson and Kris Shepherd (New York: Grand Central Publishing, 2002), 186. He was building on the definitions offered by Paul Tillich: power is "the drive of everything living to realize itself, with increasing intensity and extensity," and love is "the drive towards the unity of the separated." See Paul Tillich, *Love, Power, and Justice: Ontological Analyses and Ethical Applications* (New York: Oxford University Press, 1954), 25–26.

10. See Kahane, *Power and Love*, 88–91.

Selected Bibliography

Bentham, Jeremy B., et al. *Scenarios: An Explorer's Guide*. The Hague: Shell International, 2008.

Carvajal, Manuel José, et al. "Destino Colombia: A Scenario-Planning Process for the New Millennium." *Deeper News* 9, no. 1 (1998).

Chermack, Thomas. *Scenario Planning in Organizations: How to Create, Use, and Assess Scenarios*. San Francisco: Berrett-Koehler Publishers, 2011.

Díez Pinto, Elena, et al. *Los Escenarios del Futuro* [Scenarios of the Future]. Guatemala City, Guatemala: Visión Guatemala, 1999.

Heinzen, Barbara. *Feeling for Stones: Learning and Invention When Facing the Unknown*. London: Barbara Heinzen, 2006.

———. *How Do Societies Learn?* London: Barbara Heinzen, 2009.

———, ed. *Surviving Uncertainty*. Society for International Development. Development 47, no. 4 (2004).

Ilbury, Chantell, and Clem Sunter. *Mind of a Fox: Scenario Planning in Action*. Cape Town, South Africa: Human & Rousseau, 2001.

Kahane, Adam. *Power and Love: A Theory and Practice of Social Change*. San Francisco: Berrett-Koehler Publishers, 2009.

———. *Solving Tough Problems: An Open Way of Talking, Listening, and Creating New Realities*. San Francisco: Berrett-Koehler Publishers, 2004.

Käufer, Katrin, Glennifer Gillespie, Elena Díez Pinto, and Alfredo de León. *Learning Histories: Democratic Dialogue Regional Project*, Working Paper 3. New York: United Nations Development Programme Regional Bureau for Latin America and the Caribbean, 2004.

Kleiner, Art. *The Age of Heretics: Heroes, Outlaws, and the Forerunners of Corporate Change*. New York: Doubleday, 1996.

———. "The Man Who Saw the Future." *strategy+business* 30 (2003).

Le Roux, Pieter, Vincent Maphai, et al. "The Mont Fleur Scenarios." *Deeper News* 7, no. 1 (1992).

Ndoro, Choice, et al. *The Great Zimbabwe Scenarios: A Map of Four Possible Futures.* Harare, Zimbabwe: The Great Zimbabwe Scenarios Project, 2012.

O'Brien, William. *Character at Work: Building Prosperity Through the Practice of Virtue.* Boston: Paulist Press, 2008.

Ogilvy, James A. *Creating Better Futures: Scenario Planning as a Tool for a Better Tomorrow.* New York: Oxford University Press, 2002.

Ramírez, Rafael, John W. Selsky, and Kees van der Heijden, eds. *Business Planning for Turbulent Times: New Methods for Applying Scenarios.* London: Routledge, 2010.

Ramphele, Mamphela, et al. *The Dinokeng Scenarios: Three Futures for South Africa.* Johannesburg, South Africa: Dinokeng Scenarios, 2009.

Rettberg, Angelika. *Destino Colombia: Crónica y evaluación de un ejercicio de participación de líderes de la sociedad civil en el diseño de escenarios futuros* [Destination Colombia: Chronicle and evaluation of an exercise of civil society leaders in the design of future scenarios]. Bogotá, Colombia: Ediciones Uniandes, 2006.

Roque, Paula Cristina, and Paul-Simon Handy. *Sudan Scenarios to Strategies Workshop.* Pretoria, South Africa: Institute for Security Studies, 2010.

Santos, Juan Manuel. "Palabras del Presidente Juan Manuel Santos en la presentación del libro *Poder y Amor* de Adam Kahane" [Remarks of President Juan Manuel Santos at the presentation of the book *Power and Love*, by Adam Kahane]. Bogotá, Colombia, February 21, 2012.

———. "Presentación" [Presentation]. In Adam Kahane, *Poder y Amor: Teoría y Práctica para el Cambio Social* [Power and Love: A Theory and Practice of Social Change]. La Paz, Bolivia: Plural, 2011.

Scearce, Diana, and Katherine Fulton. *What If?: The Art of Scenario Thinking for Nonprofits.* San Francisco: Global Business Network, 2004.

Scharmer, Otto. *Theory U: Leading from the Future as It Emerges.* San Francisco: Berrett-Koehler Publishers, 2009.

Schwartz, Peter. *The Art of the Long View: Planning for the Future in an Uncertain World.* New York: Currency, 1996.

Segal, Nick. *Breaking the Mould: The Role of Scenarios in Shaping South Africa's Future.* Stellenbosch, South Africa: Sun Press, 2007.

Senge, Peter, Otto Scharmer, Joseph Jaworski, and Betty Sue Flowers. *Presence: Human Purpose and the Field of the Future.* New York: Broadway Business, 2008.

Stookey, Crane Wood. *Keep Your People in the Boat: Workforce Engagement Lessons from the Sea.* Halifax, Nova Scotia: ALIA Press, 2012.

Sunter, Clem. "The Icarus Scenario." news24.com, January 20, 2010.

———. *The World and South Africa in the 1990s.* Cape Town, South Africa: Tafelberg, 1987.

Tibbs, Hardin. "Pierre Wack: A Remarkable Source of Insight." *Netview* 9 (1998).

Tillich, Paul. *Love, Power, and Justice: Ontological Analyses and Ethical Applications.* New York: Oxford University Press, 1954.

Van der Heijden, Kees. *Scenarios: The Art of Strategic Conversation.* Chichester, West Sussex, England: John Wiley & Sons, 1996.

Van der Heijden, Kees, Ron Bradfield, George Burt, George Cairns, and George Wright. *The Sixth Sense: Accelerating Organizational Learning with Scenarios.* Chichester, West Sussex, England: John Wiley & Sons, 2002.

Wack, Pierre. "Scenarios: Shooting the Rapids" *Harvard Business Review* 63, no. 6 (1985).

———. "Scenarios: Uncharted Waters Ahead." *Harvard Business Review* 63, no. 5 (1985).

Wilkinson, Angela, and Esther Eidenow. "Evolving Practices in Environmental Scenarios: A New Scenario Typology." *Environmental Research Letters* 3 (2008).

Wilkinson, Angela, and Roland Kupers. *Re-perceiving Scenarios: The Evolution of the Gentle Art in Shell 1965–2010.* Edited by Betty Sue Flowers (forthcoming in 2012).

Wilkinson, Lawrence. "How to Build Scenarios." *Wired* (September 1995).

Zalzberg, Ofer. *EU Partnership for Peace—Israeli Track.* London: Oxford Research Group, 2009.

Acknowledgments

I HAVE HAD THE ENORMOUS GOOD FORTUNE to be able to make the journey described in this book together with many great companions.

I am indebted to the pioneers of scenario planning, who have been generous with their support, including Napier Collyns, Ged Davis, Peter Schwartz, Clem Sunter, Kees van der Heijden, and Pierre Wack.

I am grateful for the comradeship of my fellow travelers, including Antonio Aranibar, Clara Arenas, Tova Averbuch, Sarah Babb, Matt Bland, Manuel José Carvajal, David Chrislip, Daniel Coates, Ruth de Krivoy, Patrick Dodson, Betty Sue Flowers, Katherine Fulton, Pippa Green, Oscar Grossmann, Erika Gregory, Avner Haramati, Barbara Heinzen, Joseph Jaworski, Katrin Käufer, Art Kleiner, Pieter le Roux, Sarah Maddison, Arun Maira, Vincent Maphai, Debra Marsden, Ishmael Mkhabela, Joaquin Moreno, Inés de Mosquera, Nancy Murphy, Yvonne Muthien, Gustavo Mutis, Choice Ndoro, Bill O'Brien, Jay Ogilvy, Reola Phelps, Bettye Pruitt, Rafael Ramírez, Mamphela Ramphele, Tom Rautenberg, Gabrielle Rifkind, Paula Roque, Steve Rosell, Otto Scharmer, Peter Senge, Jorge Talavera, Susan Taylor, Martin Thomas, Louis van der Merwe, Margaret Vaughan, Angela Wilkinson, Alain Wouters, Shay Ben Yosef, and Ofer Zalzberg.

I have been nurtured personally and profesionally by my Reos partners, including Lenneke Aalbers, Steve Atkinson, Jeff Barnum, Marianne Mille Bøjer, Elena Díez Pinto, Mia Eisenstadt, Rebecca Freeth, Leigh Gassner, LeAnne Grillo, Gerald Harris, Zaid Hassan, Nathan Heintz, Marianne Knuth, Anaí Linares, Colleen Magner, Joe McCarron, Marcelo Michelson, Batian Nieuwerth, and Christel Scholten.

I am a member of several wonderful communities of practitioners that have given me opportunities to present and get feedback on my work in progress, including the ALIA Institute, Global Business Network, the International Futures Forum, Pegasus Communications, the Society for Organizational Learning, and the Oxford Futures Forum.

I appreciate the helpful comments on the drafts of this book, including those from Antonio Aranibar, Jeff Barnum, Marianne Mille Bøjer, Michael Crowley, Colleen Magner, Elena Díez Pinto, Mia Eisenstadt, Lorna Ely, Betty Sue Flowers, Rebecca Freeth, Leigh Gassner, LeAnne Grillo, Gerald Harris, Zaid Hassan, Elizabeth Heck, David Kahane, Art Kleiner, Marianne Knuth, Jeffrey Kulick, Pieter le Roux, Robbie MacPherson, Sarah Maddison, Colleen Magner, Trevor Manuel, Connie Matthiessen, Marcelo Michelson, Joaquin Moreno, Kristen Moussalli, Gustavo Mutis, Steve Piersanti, Rafael Ramírez, Ashley Redfield, Jeevan Sivasubramaniam, Kees van der Heijden, and Angela Wilkinson.

Finally, I want to acknowledge the loving support of my family, and especially of Dorothy.

Index

size of, 24

in South Africa's Mont Fleur
   project, 5–9

strong container and, 20, 35

summary on, 27, 97

in Zimbabwe, 27–29, 52

Wilson, Lindy, 9

Z

Zalzberg, Ofer, 42

Zimbabwe

"Chameleon" scenario on, 54

Great Zimbabwe Monument
   in, 53

scenarios for Great
   Zimbabwe Scenarios
   project, 51–54, 57, 59

"Stimela/Locomotive"
   scenario on, 53, 54

"Stone People" scenario on,
   53, 54

suspending process by
   scenario team in, 93

uncertainties in, 51–52

"Vulture State" scenario on,
   53, 54

whole-system team for Great
   Zimbabwe Scenarios
   project, 27–29, 52

About Reos Partners

REOS PARTNERS is a social innovation consultancy that addresses complex, high-stakes challenges around the world.

We design and facilitate processes that enable teams of stakeholders—even those who don't understand or trust one another—to work together to make progress on their toughest problems.

We work on issues such as employment, health, food, energy, the environment, security, and peace. We partner with governments, corporations, and civil society organizations.

Our approach is systemic, creative, and participative.

We are guides more than advisors. We are experienced at helping diverse groups navigate through uncharted territory to reach their most important goals.

We work both locally and globally. We have offices in Cambridge (Massachusetts), Johannesburg, Melbourne, Oxford, São Paulo, San Francisco, and The Hague.

www.reospartners.com

About the Author

ADAM KAHANE has been working with the future for 30 years, in three phases. He started off trying to forecast the future. He trained as a scientist, with an undergraduate degree in physics from McGill University in Montreal and a graduate degree in energy and resources from the University of California in Berkeley. He held research positions at the University of British Columbia in Vancouver, the International Institute for Applied Systems Analysis in Vienna, the Organisation for Economic Co-operation and Development in Paris, and the Institute for Energy Economics in Tokyo. He learned that it is not possible to forecast much—that the future is filled with surprises.

This motivated Adam to enter his second phase. He wanted to get involved in real-world decision making about how to survive and thrive in such conditions of uncertainty. He got a job as a corporate planning coordinator at Pacific Gas and Electric Company in San Francisco. Then he joined the Group Planning department of Royal Dutch Shell in London. Shell's legendary scenario planning team helped the company to develop robust strategies by constructing multiple stories of possible futures. Adam became head of global social, political, economic, environmental, and technological scenarios.

While he was at Shell, Adam had an unexpected opportunity to lead a diverse team of South African leaders who were trying to shape the transition away from apartheid—the Mont Fleur Scenario Exercise. This remarkable experience catapulted him into his third phase: working not on forecasting or adapting to the future but on transforming it. Since then, he has led such transformative scenario planning projects in tens of countries all over the world. He has worked with many diverse teams of leaders trying to address their toughest challenges, including executives and politicians, generals and guerrillas, civil servants and trade unionists, community activists and United Nations officials, clergy and artists.

Adam has cofounded several organizations to advance the practice and theory of transformative scenario planning; the most recent of these is Reos Partners. Adam also teaches scenario planning at the Saïd Business School of the University of Oxford and is a member of Global Business Network, the International Futures Forum, and the World Academy of Art and Science. Along the way, he earned a master's degree in applied behavioral science from Bastyr University and studied negotiation at Harvard Law School and cello performance at Institut Marguerite-Bourgeoys.

Adam and his wife, Dorothy, have four children and seven grandchildren and so are heavily invested in the future. They live in Cape Town and Montreal.

kahane@reospartners.com

Also by Adam Kahane

Power and Love
A Theory and Practice of Social Change

The two methods frequently employed to solve our toughest social problems—either violence and aggression or endless negotiation and compromise—are fundamentally flawed. This is because the seemingly contradictory drives behind these approaches—*power*, the desire to achieve one's purpose, and *love*, the urge to unite with others—are actually complementary. As Dr. Martin Luther King Jr. put it, "Power without love is reckless and abusive, and love without power is sentimental and anemic."

Adam Kahane delves deeply into the dual natures of both power and love and relates how, through trial and error, he has learned to balance them, offering practical guidance for how others can learn that balance as well.

Paperback, 192 pages, ISBN 978-1-60509-304-8
PDF ebook, ISBN 978-1-60509-305-5

BK Berrett–Koehler Publishers, Inc.
San Francisco, *www.bkconnection.com*   **800.929.2929**

Also by Adam Kahane

Solving Tough Problems

An Open Way of Talking, Listening, and Creating New Realities

"This breakthrough book addresses the central challenge of our time: finding a way to work together to solve the problems we have created."

—Nelson Mandela

Adam Kahane has worked on some of the most difficult problems in the world, from post-apartheid South Africa to Colombia during the civil war, Guatemala after the genocide, Israel-Palestine, Northern Ireland, Cyprus, and the Basque Country. Through these experiences, he has learned how to create environments that enable innovative new ideas and solutions to emerge and be implemented even in the most challenging contexts. Here Kahane tells his stories and distills from them an approach that all of us can use to solve our own toughest problems.

Paperback, 168 pages, ISBN 978-1-57675-464-1
PDF ebook, ISBN 978-1-57675-537-2

BK Berrett–Koehler Publishers, Inc.
San Francisco, *www.bkconnection.com*   **800.929.2929**

Berrett–Koehler
Publishers

Berrett-Koehler is an independent publisher dedicated to an ambitious mission: *Creating a World That Works for All.*

We believe that to truly create a better world, action is needed at all levels—individual, organizational, and societal. At the individual level, our publications help people align their lives with their values and with their aspirations for a better world. At the organizational level, our publications promote progressive leadership and management practices, socially responsible approaches to business, and humane and effective organizations. At the societal level, our publications advance social and economic justice, shared prosperity, sustainability, and new solutions to national and global issues.

A major theme of our publications is "Opening Up New Space." Berrett-Koehler titles challenge conventional thinking, introduce new ideas, and foster positive change. Their common quest is changing the underlying beliefs, mindsets, institutions, and structures that keep generating the same cycles of problems, no matter who our leaders are or what improvement programs we adopt.

We strive to practice what we preach—to operate our publishing company in line with the ideas in our books. At the core of our approach is stewardship, which we define as a deep sense of responsibility to administer the company for the benefit of all of our "stakeholder" groups: authors, customers, employees, investors, service providers, and the communities and environment around us.

We are grateful to the thousands of readers, authors, and other friends of the company who consider themselves to be part of the "BK Community." We hope that you, too, will join us in our mission.

A BK Currents Book

This book is part of our BK Currents series. BK Currents books advance social and economic justice by exploring the critical intersections between business and society. Offering a unique combination of thoughtful analysis and progressive alternatives, BK Currents books promote positive change at the national and global levels. To find out more, visit **www.bkconnection.com**.

Berrett–Koehler
Publishers

A community dedicated to creating
a world that works for all

Visit Our Website: www.bkconnection.com

Read book excerpts, see author videos and Internet movies, read
our authors' blogs, join discussion groups, download book apps, find
out about the BK Affiliate Network, browse subject-area libraries of
books, get special discounts, and more!

Subscribe to Our Free E-Newsletter, the *BK Communiqué*

Be the first to hear about new publications, special discount offers,
exclusive articles, news about bestsellers, and more! Get on the list
for our free e-newsletter by going to **www.bkconnection.com**.

Get Quantity Discounts

Berrett-Koehler books are available at quantity discounts for orders
of ten or more copies. Please call us toll-free at (800) 929-2929 or
email us at bkp.orders@aidcvt.com.

Join the BK Community

BKcommunity.com is a virtual meeting place where people from
around the world can engage with kindred spirits to create a world
that works for all. BKcommunity.com members may create their own
profiles, blog, start and participate in forums and discussion groups,
post photos and videos, answer surveys, announce and register for
upcoming events, and chat with others online in real time. Please join
the conversation!